How High can a Kangaroo Hop?

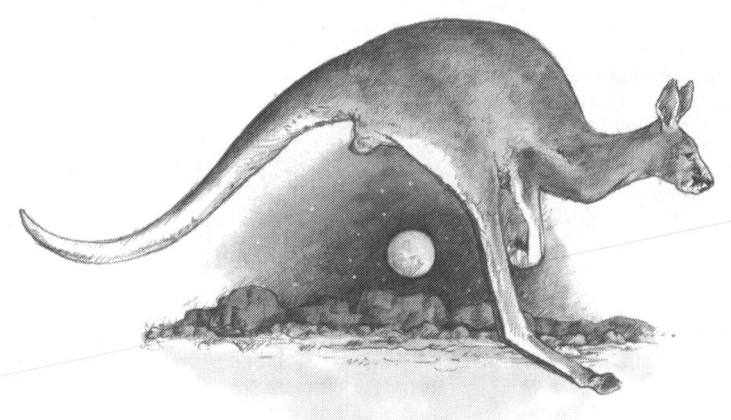

JACKIE FRENCH
illustrated by BRUCE WHATLEY

An imprint of HarperCollins*Publishers*

Angus&Robertson
An imprint of HarperCollins*Publishers*, Australia

First published in Australia in 2008
by HarperCollins*Publishers* Australia Pty Limited
ABN 36 009 913 517
www.harpercollins.com.au

Text copyright © Jackie French 2008
Illustrations copyright © Farmhouse Illustration Company Pty Ltd 2008

The right of Jackie French to be identified as the author and Brucke Whatley as the illustrator of this work has been asserted by them under the *Copyright Amendment (Moral Rights) Act 2000*.

This work is copyright.
Apart from any use as permitted under the *Copyright Act 1968*, no part may be reproduced, copied, scanned, stored in a retrieval system, recorded, or transmitted, in any form or by any means, without the prior written permission of the publisher.

HarperCollins*Publishers*
25 Ryde Road, Pymble, Sydney NSW 2073, Australia
31 View Road, Glenfield, Auckland 10, New Zealand
1–A, Hamilton House, Connaught Place, New Delhi – 110 001, India
77–85 Fulham Palace Road, London W6 8JB, United Kingdom
2 Bloor Street East, 20th floor, Toronto, Ontario M4W 1A8, Canada
10 East 53rd Street, New York NY 10022, USA

National Library of Australia Cataloguing-in-publication data:

Author: French, Jackie.
Title: How high can a kangaroo hop?
Author: Jackie French; illustrator, Bruce Whatley.
Publisher: Pymble, N.S.W. : Harper Collins Publishers, 2008.
ISBN: 978 07322 8544 9 (pbk.)
Notes: Includes index.
Target Audience: For primary school age.
Subjects: Kangaroos–Australia–Juvenile literature.
         Wallabies–Australia–Juvenile literature.
Other Authors/Contributors: Whatley, Bruce.
Dewey Number: 599.22

Cover design by Matt Stanton
Cover and internal illustrations by Bruce Whatley
Typeset in 12 on 17 Esprit Book by Helen Beard, ECJ Australia Pty Limited
Printed and bound in Australia by Griffin Press
79gsm Bulky Paperback used by HarperCollins*Publishers* is a natural, recyclable product made from wood grown in a combination of sustainable plantation and regrowth forests. It also contains up to a 20% portion of recycled fibre. The manufacturing processes conform to the environmental regulations in Tasmania, the place of manufacture.

5 4 3 2 1   08 09 10 11

To Rosies, Bounce, Flounce, Biceps, Harry, Josephine, Hopalong, Freds One, Two and Three, Pratt, House Mouse, Fuschia, Nuisance, Giganticus and all the other 'big foots' who have shared their lives with us.

Contents

1 Welcome to a most amazing world 1

   Amazing roos 5
   Kangaroo basics 7
   Mysterious marsupials 8
   'Big foots' 8
   Are you a kangaroo? 10
   The story of the wallaby gourmet 11

2 From lost giants to the modern roo 17

   The lost giants of Australia 17
   Monster roos! 18
   The story of Jo Jo 22

3 Kangaroos and the indigenous people 25

   Hunting kangaroos 25
   How to hunt a wallaby 30
   Living 'sustainably' so the land keeps providing 31
   Smart farming 33
   What to do with a dead kangaroo 33
   How to make an earth oven 34
   How to make a kangaroo-skin rug or cloak 38
   How Europeans saw their first roos 39

Did the Chinese find roos? 40
How roos and wallabies got their names 41
What's in a name? 45
Roo stew and other colonial yum-yums 46
How roos and some wallabies recovered 48
Our first national park 50
Boxing kangaroos 51

4 What roo is that? 53
The Eastern Grey — the most common roo 54
Could *you* box a kangaroo? 57
The Western Grey — a most smelly roo 59
The big Red — the most muscular roo 60
The Red-necked Wallaby — a roo, too 63
The Swamp Wallaby — the worst manners 65
The story of Harry 69
The story of breakfast with Rosie 77
The Tree-kangaroo — a most amazing roo 80
The Quokka — the cutest roo of all! 85
The Rock Wallabies — rare endangered species 89
Amazing lost wallaby colonies 97
Extinct wallabies that aren't! 98

5 A night-time roo adventure 105
Down at the creek 109

6 Roos growing up — 121

   Breeding and birth — 122
   Life inside the pouch — 124
   A world outside the pouch — 127
   A most incredible type of milk — 128

7 Fascinating roo poo — 131

   The beetles with too much poo to chew — 132
   Roo poo is useful — 132
   How to handle roo poo — 135
   What roo poo is that? — 136
   Make a poo collection — 139

8 How to move like a kangaroo — 141

   Boundless energy — 141
   Horsepower or roo-power? — 144
   Deciphering roo and wallaby tracks — 146
   The amazing surfing roos — 148
   Staying cool like a kangaroo — 148
   The story of roos who came in from the cold — 151

9 Roos and you — 155

   Where kangaroos hang out — 155
   The story of the salad sandwiches — 157
   Good manners around roos and wallabies — 162
   What to do if a roo attacks — 166

10 How to watch roos and wallabies safely — 167
    Locating roos and wallabies in your area — 168
    How to find your way around at night — 171
    How to avoid scaring roos and wallabies away — 173
    The short story of walking with wallabies — 178

11 Caring for orphan joeys — 179
    What to do with an orphaned or injured joey — 180
    The story of Nuisance — 185

12 Protecting our roos and wallabies — 191
    Roos on the road — 192
    Living with roos on farms — 192
    Keeping a roo as a pet — 195
    There's a wallaby in my garden — 196
    The story of the dancing kangaroo — 199

Roo phrases — 205
Roo and wallaby jokes — 209
Who's who of wallabies and roos — 215

Index — 232

1

Welcome to a most amazing world

Australia has some extraordinary animals — different from all other animals in the world. That's because our animals have been isolated from animals in other countries for at least 45 million years. Originally, Australia, Antarctica and South America were joined together and had the same animals; animals which were the ancestors of modern marsupials (more about marsupials later ...). But then this big landmass broke up into the different continents we know today and Australia was left on its own as a big island.

Australia's animals had to evolve without any contact with the rest of the world, except for New Guinea, which was joined onto Australia till about

8000 years ago, when the seas rose after the last Ice Age. And that is what makes them so unique.

Australia's animals had to be tough. At times in its history Australia was very wet and the animals that evolved were suited to those conditions. But today, most of Australia is desert. Even in wet areas there are often years with little rain. Droughts can last hundreds or even thousands of years. What kind of animals can survive a land like this?

Ones that can hop, instead of walk. Our kangaroos and wallabies can move more efficiently than any other animal on Earth.

Hopping helps kangaroos and wallabies travel to new places to feed in a land that can be dry for years, and then suddenly turn green and lush. Roos and wallabies have massive tummies for storing food too. And in bad times they can live on dry grass or leaves that few other animals could live on. Many can go for hundreds of kilometres with little or even no water, just on the moisture in their food.

When their land is dry and drought stricken, roos and wallabies can delay their unborn babies from developing until the rains and grass return again. But in good times they can breed quickly, to make the most of the lush grass before the sun turns the land brown again.

Some roos can climb trees. Others can swim, or leap from rock to rock. The largest roos of all can leap nine metres in a single bound! And all female roos have pouches for carrying their babies and they don't fall out, either (well, most of the time, anyway!).

Our kangaroos and wallabies are incredible! So why don't we yell '*Amazing!*' whenever we see a roo or wallaby?

Because we're used to them. We see roos in advertising, or on television shows. Sporting teams are named after them. Hardly a day goes by when we don't hear the word 'roo' or 'wallaby'.

Yet even though the kangaroo is one of our national emblems, most Australians have never lived with kangaroos. Most know very little about these extraordinary creatures that share this country with us.

I'm lucky. I've lived with roos and wallabies and other wildlife most of my life. The roos keep the grass short around our house, and the wallabies eat my roses and wake me up as they pound past my bedroom at two in the morning. One of the most wonderful things in my life is being able to walk among wild animals who accept me as part of their world.

But these days fewer and fewer people can share the lives of roos and wallabies. Every night thousands of roos and wallabies are killed on our roads. Many farmers still consider roos or wallabies as pests, and believe that they should be destroyed. They have never even tried to find ways to farm with wildlife. Many wallabies such as the Bridled Nail-tail Wallaby and the Yellow-footed Rock Wallaby are endangered, and may become extinct in the next ten years because much of their land has been taken away from them, and feral animals eat their food or kill their babies. But if we care enough, humans and roos and wallabies *can* share this land.

And that's why I wrote this book: to share with you this fascinating world of one of the most incredible animals in the universe, and hope that you, too, will help find ways for wild animals and humans to live together.

Amazing roos

- A male kangaroo is called a boomer. Male roos can fight each other for three days and nights, only stopping when they drop from exhaustion.
- A female kangaroo is called a flyer. Mother roos and wallabies can feed three babies at the same time — and give each one of them a different sort of milk. (No, not chocolate flavoured!)
- A baby kangaroo is called a joey. A joey will eat its mother's droppings because they contain tiny organisms from the mother's gut that will help the joey digest grass. Without them the joey might get diarrhoea and even die.

Mother would can feed three babies at the same time, each on a different kind of milk. (No, not chocolate flavoured!)

Kangaroo basics

The basic difference between a kangaroo and a wallaby is that a roo is big and a wallaby is small. But there are lots of differences between the many types (called species) of roos and wallabies.

Big Red Kangaroos can stand nearly two metres tall and weigh around one hundred kilograms. But wallabies like the Nabarlek are tiny and delicate and weigh less than a kilogram.

Many species of roos and wallabies live in groups called mobs. Sometimes there are great mobs of fifty or even more than a hundred roos, all munching grass together. But other species mostly live by themselves unless they have a baby. Some species, like the Red-necked Wallaby, live in small groups of five or ten.

Different roos and wallabies eat different foods, too. Kangaroos eat almost nothing but grass, or grass-like crops like young oats or wheat. Some wallabies mostly eat grass too, but other wallabies like the Black-tailed Wallaby, only eat grass if there's nothing tastier around! They use their paws to pull down vines and suck them up like spaghetti. They also eat young leaves or shoots and love to taste new foods.

Kangaroos mostly like flat plains or open forest. Most wallabies like shrubs and shelter. But when times are bad roos will move into the denser forest country, and other wallabies like prefer open grassy places.

Different kangaroo and wallaby species vary enormously in size, from giant 'big Reds' to the tiny Warabi

 **Fact**
Even though kangaroos and wallabies are only found naturally in the wild in Australia and New Guinea, some have been taken by animal collectors and gone wild in New Zealand, Great Britain and Hawaii.

Mysterious marsupials

Kangaroos and wallabies are marsupials. Marsupials give birth to their young when they're very small and not fully developed. The tiny baby keeps growing attached to a teat on the outside of its mum's body. Most marsupials — but not all — have pouches where the baby lives.

Many people think that they are only found in Australia because there are so many marsupials here. But there are also marsupials in North and South America, and lots in New Guinea. Although they had the same ancestors as Australian marsupials they have evolved into quite different animals. Marsupial fossils have even been found in Europe and Asia.

'Big foots'

Kangaroos and wallabies belong to a group of marsupials called 'macropods', which means 'big foot'. All roos and wallabies have the strong back legs

Kangaroos bound on powerful back legs and use their tail for balance

and long, long back feet that give their family its name. They bound on their enormous back legs, using their tail for balance (to give them a little extra oomph!) and use their front legs for support. It's possibly the most energy-efficient way of travelling long distances in the world.

A kangaroo or wallaby can't walk like we do, going from one foot to the other foot, just like we can't bound like a kangaroo. Humans can jump, leap and hop, but it's very difficult to give more than a few bounds without falling over.

Are you a kangaroo?

🐾 Are you hairy all over, except for under your feet and your nose? Well, you might be a roo . . . or just a really hairy human.

🐾 Do you cool yourself down by licking your paws? (If you do I really hope you *are* a kangaroo!)

🐾 Do you have a pouch if you're a girl?

🐾 Can you jump over a fence in a single bound, or leap twenty times without falling over?

🐾 Even better, can you bound twenty kilometres without stopping or having a drink?

If you answered 'yes' to all these questions, then . . . congratulations! You're either a kangaroo or a really weird hairy kid who's going to win every long-distance event at the next Olympics.

 Fact

Roos have tough feet. But sometimes kangaroos and wallabies *do* get splinters or big thorns in their feet, and the foot can become infected. The infection can even kill them. But many roos who can only use one foot still manage to move slowly by balancing on their tails, and survive for years like that too.

The story of the wallaby gourmet

I met my first kangaroo forty-five years ago, when he chased my baby sister around the kangaroo enclosure at the local wildlife park to pinch her peanut butter sandwich.

The roo was cute and it was funny. (Well, I thought it was funny. I don't think my baby sister did.) And that's pretty much all I thought about roos, until one day when I was nineteen.

We were driving from Brisbane to take up new jobs in Canberra. We drove through brown hills and lots of flies, and I thought, 'If this is the inland it's the most boring place on Earth. Give me a nice mangrove swamp any day.'

Then suddenly the sun came out. The hills turned gold. And there, sweeping across the slope, was a mob of roos, between thirty to fifty of them, like a melody of fur and beauty.

I fell in love.

I realised hills didn't have to be green and lush to be beautiful.

This was a new world. I wanted to know it and understand it. And I had a feeling that the way to do this was to get to know these amazing, leaping creatures.

A couple of years after that I moved to the farm in the valley where I live now. It's mostly bush, on the edge of a wilderness area.

I expected to be living with kangaroos, but there weren't any, at least for the first few years. Our end of the valley is too steep and bushy for roos. They only move up here when it's dry, and they're hunting for grass and water.

So the first 'big foot' I lived with wasn't one of those great big, graceful creatures. It was a wallaby called Fred, with small, rounded shoulders and a long black tail that poked out whenever he hid from visitors behind the fence. Fred always thought that as long as he couldn't see humans, then they couldn't see him . . . so he never bothered to hide his tail.

'Snake! Snake!' the visitors would cry. And I'd say, 'Don't worry. That's just Fred.'

I called him Fred because he lived by the shed, where I lived in those days. I first met him in my new vegie garden.

'Oh look,' I thought. 'How sweet! There's a dear little wallaby in my garden.' And then I thought, 'That dear little wallaby is eating my lettuces!'

'Get out of it, you hairy dingbat!' I yelled.

Fred looked up at me for a second, then went back to the lettuces. He thought my new vegie garden was a wonderful idea. First he took a bite of carrot top, then a bite of lettuce. Then he'd nibble some onion, and then went back to the lettuce.

I put a fence around the vegie garden the next day. By then there weren't many lettuces left, and the carrots and the onions had a chewed look too.

Fred liked oranges, as well. He picked them from the trees, holding them with both hands while he bit into the ripe fruit, slurping at the juice as it ran down his fur. He loved mandarins, and even lemons, though he only took a bite or two of those, crinkling up his face at the sourness. He adored apricots and peaches; in fact, every fruit or vegetable I grew.

And then he discovered my rubbish bucket.

I kept the rubbish bucket outside the shed door. Every morning I took the apple cores and bread crusts and other scraps to the chooks. But one morning Fred was there first. When I came out he was holding a piece of pineapple peel. There was pineapple juice all down his front, and on his face was a look of total joy. Fred had found a new fruit! I didn't have the heart to disturb him.

After the pineapple Fred tried a crust of toast and marmalade. Toast and marmalade was even better than the pineapple. He tasted some potato peel, but didn't like it. But when Fred bit into some squishy rockmelon he looked like he'd found paradise.

Fred and I lived together for years. I cried when he finally died of old age. But by the next

morning another wallaby had moved into Fred's territory to take his place.

At the moment we have six wallabies living near our house. (I've planted lots of fruit trees and gardens in the last thirty years, so there's enough food for a lot more wildlife now than when I first came here.)

My favourite wallaby is Rosie. She's so used to us that she doesn't even bound away when I yell, 'Stop eating my roses!' In fact, I don't even bother yelling at her now. Rosie is a delicate eater and even if she nibbles the leaves, the bushes grow back again.

But they don't when Biceps munches them. Biceps is a male. He grabs the branches and bends them till they snap. Luckily Biceps only comes up close to the house — and the roses — during droughts, when there isn't much else about to eat.

Then there's Bounce, one of Rosie's daughters, who still likes to hang about near mum; and House Mouse, who was still pale grey and almost hairless when she first hopped out of the pouch, just like a jumping mouse. There's Big Bum, too, who was so lazy he didn't leave Rosie's pouch till he was so big it dragged on the ground, and down by the car shed Hop-a-long still manages to hop on one leg. She hurt her foot somehow years ago, so it's withered and pretty useless now. But Hop-a-long still has a good life eating the fallen apples and avocadoes, fruit tree leaves and grass near the creek.

I meet all of them early every morning when I go for my walk, and watch them from our windows too. We have big windows in every room, even the bathroom (there's no one except the wallabies and wombats to peer in at us), so it's easy to spy on the wildlife. The wildlife think we're a nuisance sometimes, especially when we have visitors who wake them up when they're dozing under the avocado trees. But they're mostly pretty tolerant of the stupid things humans get up to, like making a noise with chainsaws to cut firewood, or picking half the apricots — the ones that they, and the rosellas and possums, have left us.

And it *is* a new world. It's been a fascinating one, living here with roos and wallabies and other wildlife, just as I thought all those years ago.

2

From lost giants to the modern roo

We don't know who saw the first kangaroos in Australia — Aboriginal history wasn't written down, and the places where the first humans arrived in Australia 40,000 to 60,000 years ago are probably now underwater, as sea levels are higher now than they were then.

But we do know that when the first humans arrived in Australia, they saw a terrifying creature, with fangs and claws. It was one of the earliest kangaroos.

The lost giants of Australia
The Giant Short-faced Kangaroo (*Procoptodon goliah*) wasn't just tall (about three metres high) and furry. It

bounded along on its two back legs, balancing with its tail, and it had big claws on its feet and hands . . .

Procoptodon was dangerous, even though it only used its claws to pull down branches to eat leaves, and *it* didn't have fangs. But you wouldn't have wanted to make one angry. You want those nice berries over there? Well, you just go ahead . . . and you can have mine, too.

Monster roos!

Scientists have discovered the fossils of twenty-three species of giant roo in caves in the hot, treeless Nullarbor Plain. They lived about 800,000 years ago. Some of the roos were three times bigger than big Red Kangaroos. There were also two species of tree kangaroo and a weird wallaby with an overhanging forehead.

A team of palaeontologists from the University of New South Wales have also dug up fossils of a 'killer' Rat-Kangaroo at Riversleigh in northwest Queensland. The 'killer' Rat-Kangaroo lived in the Riversleigh region somewhere between ten million and twenty million years ago. It was about the size of a sheep dog, and it galloped instead of hopped. It had long teeth like a wolf's for ripping flesh and heavy jaws for crunching through bones.

A Giant Short-faced Kangaroo wonders what to eat for breakfast

There were other giant creatures in those days too, like the rhinoceros-sized, wombat-like *Diprotodons*, huge carnivorous goannas, marsupial lions and five-metre-long pythons — all probably even more terrifying than the giant roos.

Procoptodons died out about 40,000 years ago, but the massive beast was an ancestor of our modern kangaroos. But by about 10,000 years ago, every creature larger than a human had vanished.

What happened to our lost giants? Did the big animals die out as the land grew colder and drier during the last Ice Age and there wasn't enough food for giant creatures? Did the big animals starve when people began to manage the land with fire? Or did humans hunt so many of them that they all died out? Maybe it was a combination — we need more information to really know.

Even though all of these giant animals died out, their smaller relatives survived. Perhaps they were faster and could run away from humans with spears, or were smaller, like wombats, and could hide in holes. Maybe because they were smaller they didn't need so much food in the drier, harsh land that Australia had become.

So, even though we don't have giant kangaroos any more, we still do have at least sixty-nine different species of kangaroos and wallabies.

Living fossil

One ancient species of wallaby that *has* survived from about four million years ago to the present is the Agile Wallaby (*Macropus agilis*).

In ancient times the Agile Wallaby was a bit bigger than it is today (we can tell this from fossils found at Chinchilla, Queensland). But otherwise it's just the same.

How did this wallaby survive when so many of its relatives died, or evolved into other species?

The Agile Wallaby grazes in open forests as well as on native grass on sand dunes; maybe this wallaby could adapt to many different areas when times were bad or the climate changed.

The story of Jo Jo

The first real 'roo' I ever met, well, socially, was called Jo Jo. I'd been to a lecture in Canberra on the giant megafauna. It was cold and late, so a friend asked me if I'd like to stay the night at their place and drive home in the morning.

I sat by their fire in the living room and dreamed of all the creatures I'd just heard about: the rhino-sized wombats, the giant roos with fangs . . .

Suddenly two furry hands pushed the door open. A furry face peered in. A furry something made three neat bounds, then jumped down the neck of my jumper. It turned a somersault and suddenly its small, furry face peered up at me as though to say, 'Ah, now we're both comfortable, aren't we?'

It didn't look anything like the giant creature I'd been dreaming about.

My friend Helen looked in. 'I hope you don't mind Jo Jo.'

'No,' I said politely, trying to look as if I were used to baby kangaroos leaping down my jumper. 'He's fine.'

Jo Jo decided he liked being down my jumper. He stayed there while Helen handed me his bottle. His two tiny, furry hands helped me hold it as I fed him. Then he snuggled down on my lap and slept while we all ate dinner.

I fed him another bottle of milk again later. I was sleepy, but Jo Jo was just getting ready to play. He raced around the kitchen, down the hall, through the living room, hopped onto the sofa, hopped onto a chair, hopped onto the table, then bounded into the bathroom and back to the kitchen. He looked at us as though to say, 'Come on! It's night! It's time to have fun!'

'He'll settle down when we've gone to bed,' said Helen.

I woke up at 4.30 am next morning to find that I was sharing my bed with two small children, one bouncing kangaroo and the cat. Jo Jo wanted his breakfast. The kids just wanted to help him bounce. At seven the cat and I got up. The others went back to sleep.

Jo Jo bounded out for breakfast a little later. I fed him his bottle while Helen made scrambled eggs. Then he leapt back into the hessian bag pouch that hung from one of the chairs.

We might be just starting our day, but Jo Jo had had a busy night, and he was tired.

'Is he always like that?' I asked Helen.

'Always,' she said. 'There's nothing like looking after a wild animal. Nothing at all.'

I looked back at Jo Jo. All I could see now was a large lump in the pouch.

I had met my first baby kangaroo. And it was love.

3

Kangaroos and the indigenous people

When the Aboriginal nations were broken up after white settlers arrived and took over their lands, much of their history and stories were lost. But we know that the kangaroo was important to their history — though maybe not quite as important as many people think.

Hunting kangaroos

In many places the main meat indigenous people ate was kangaroo, at least at certain times of the year. Roos were only hunted by men. But meat was only a small part of the indigenous people's food a lot of the time. The food women gathered was even more important — mainly grains from wild grasses and tussocks, and tubers like myrrnong daisy yams. (Just like these days we eat more bread and pasta and vegies than meat — or we should!) The women also caught birds and reptiles.

Aboriginal clans along the coast ate more fish and shellfish than meat. Kangaroos moved around with the seasons, too, so they weren't always easily spotted. And they were very hard to catch.

Kangaroos move fast, and they have scouts that watch for people or animals who might hurt them. As soon as the warning thud or grunt is heard the entire mob leaps away, often moving in several directions to make it harder for hunters to catch more than one at a time.

So in some places in Australia possum meat or ducks or fish were eaten more often than kangaroo. (It's easy to

The scout is always on the lookout for potential threats to the mob

catch a possum when it's sleeping in a tree hollow during the day, or to swim under a duck to grab its legs; well, easier than catching a bounding kangaroo, anyhow.)

No animals were hunted for fun, or sport — it was always for food, and everyone had to obey very strict laws about hunting. The indigenous people believed that animals like kangaroos and wallabies were descended from the same great ancestors as humans, for example, and there were individual indigenous people who were raised to regard certain animals as their particular ancestor. Those who considered the kangaroo as their ancestor were never allowed to kill or eat kangaroo at all.

In other places hunting and killing a kangaroo single-handedly then bringing it back to the camp was one of the first initiations for a boy to pass as part of his manhood training. A good hunter was admired and looked up to by fellow men and boys in the clan.

The indigenous people were experts at many different ways to hunt kangaroos. Sometimes hundreds of men from many clans would gather for a kangaroo hunt. They slowly circled the mob, then all cast their spears together, or used spear throwers to make the spears go further and penetrate the animal more deeply. In other places boomerangs were thrown to hit the roos on the neck or head, stunning them so that the hunters could run closer to spear them.

The hunters would be totally silent as they stalked the roos, using hand signals to tell each other where to go or what to do next, though sometimes whistles were used too. Hunters made sure that they were downwind from the roos, too, so that the animals couldn't smell them. Sometimes hunters rubbed themselves with yellow ochre all over, so that they'd blend in with the dry golden-coloured grass. The ochre also helped disguise the smell of human, especially if it was rubbed thickly under the hunter's arms where they might sweat in the heat. Wood ash could be rubbed on the skin too, or orange clay.

Sometimes one man acted as a decoy. He'd attract the kangaroos' attention, then while they were looking at him and wondering what he was doing the other hunters would creep closer, freezing whenever the roos glanced their way.

Fact

Aboriginal hunters knew how to stand so that the roos didn't realise they were people. They might stand on one leg, perhaps, with the other bent so they didn't look like a two-legged human, or next to a tree or bush that would disguise their shape. They would never look directly at a kangaroo either, only sideways, or with their head bent on their chest. (Kangaroos are very good at picking out human faces.)

The hunt was men's business, though sometimes women and children helped. In some places men and women made big fences from sticks and branches, and then drove the kangaroos towards them until they were trapped against the fence and could be speared by hunters. On the New England tablelands of New South Wales men and women made great nets and hung them between the trees to catch wallabies and roos.

In Central Australia people dug pit traps — big holes covered with branches and grass — so the animals would fall into them as they ran from the hunters. Sometimes people drugged waterholes with the roots or leaves of plants. Any animal that drank there would fall asleep, and could be caught.

In the lower Blue Mountains of New South Wales many clans joined together to hunt kangaroos. They formed an enormous circle, one or even two kilometres wide, with about twenty metres between each person. Everyone held a handful of burning bark and, at a signal, lit the grass and bush in front of them. The kangaroos or wallabies inside the circle fled further inside the circle to escape from the fire. The hunters followed, slipping between the burning areas, yelling as loudly as they could to terrify the animals even further. Then as the desperate animals tried to escape through the line of hunters, they'd be speared.

How to hunt a wallaby

If you wanted to catch a wallaby you needed to know what its tracks looked like, or where it drank at dusk. Aboriginal people knew which route migrating wallabies followed when they moved from summer to winter feeding grounds. Hunters hid behind rocks to catch wallabies unawares, or tracked them for many kilometres, studying how fast the animals were moving by the pattern of their footprints to work out how fast they were moving and how long it had been since they'd left the tracks so they would know if they could catch up to them or not.

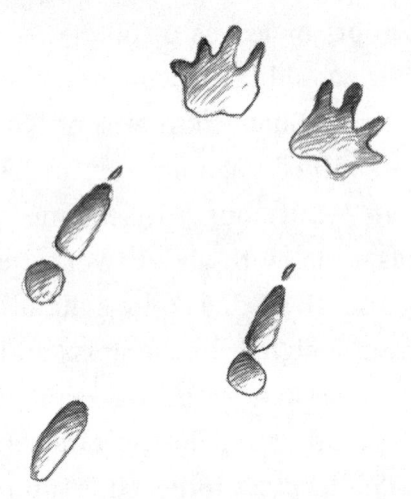

The prints from this roo shows it's been hoping along to feed. You can see where it's been resting on its tail and hands.

In the Tumut area of New South Wales men rubbed themselves with charcoal and pretended to be a tree by the river. When the roos came to drink they speared or clubbed them to death. After dingoes arrived in Australia about 4,000 to 5,000 years ago, they were trained to help hunt kangaroos too.

Living 'sustainably' so the land keeps providing
One of the main ways indigenous people maintained a good supply of roos was the use of 'fire-stick farming' — burning the land to encourage new, lush grass to spring up. This was one of the most important tools that the indigenous people used to ensure that there was food, not just for the next month, but for the next decade.

When grassland is burnt the new grass is irresistible to roos. Most native grasses are pretty tough, so soft green grass was extra yum.

This meant that the indigenous people could attract mobs of roos whenever they wanted them. But fire-stick farming also meant that different parts of the land were used for food every year. Only small patches of land were ever burnt at any one time — and never great big fires, like today's bushfires, that destroy trees or bake the land so hard that grass and other plants wouldn't grow.

Land that was burnt every few years was easier to travel through, and made it easier to see animal tracks, too.

Except in areas up in the Torres Strait to the north of Australia the indigenous people didn't farm the land by digging and planting, which was the way other people did it in Europe, Africa, the Americas or parts of Asia. Instead, they managed the land itself, so it would keep providing for them.

Australian droughts can go on in some areas for ten or even twenty years, not just for a year or two. So in the pioneering days before fridges and trucks it was desperately important to know how to ensure that the land could continually feed you.

The best fruits were left so that their seeds would grow more fruit trees or bushes. The Aboriginal people also used 'living larders' — areas that were only used when food was scarce.

In some regions like the Finke River near Alice Springs food was only hunted or collected from some places in severe droughts, so that there would always be food even in very bad times.

> **Fact**
>
> Other foods, like ant larvae, were only eaten in drought too — not because they didn't taste good, but to make sure there'd be plenty of food even when there was no grass to feed roos nearby. (Some ants can taste almost as sweet as lollies, or as rich and nutty as peanut butter.)

Smart farming

Most of Australia's soil is 'old'. It hasn't been burped out of a volcano or left by floods or glaciers. It's often high in salt, too, from hundreds of thousands of years of wind blowing in from the sea. Mostly, it's just not suited to European farming methods, with lots of ploughing. Even today a farm can lose six tonnes of soil for every tonne of wheat it grows — the soil just washes or blows away. So fire-stick farming was a superb way to ensure that the land kept on providing food.

What to do with a dead kangaroo
Warning!
Don't read this if you're soft-hearted (or squeamish)!

Once a kangaroo (or wallaby) was speared the hunters rushed up. If the animal was still alive, they gave it a sharp blow on the neck, which killed it instantly.

The hunters then made a small hole in the abdomen of the dead kangaroo, and poked a stick inside it. They twirled the stick around expertly to gather up the guts so that they could be pulled out. At other times they might make a bigger hole to lift out the guts in one piece. This way they could stuff the stomach or bladder with grass or feathers to make a ball for children to play games with.

After the guts were taken out the hunter that had speared the roo carried it home over his shoulders in triumph. Back at the camp he threw it onto a hot blazing fire to singe off the fur, then took it off again. Then the proper cooking began.

How to make an earth oven

1. Dig a pit, at least a metre deep.
2. Line it with stones.
3. Fill the pit with wood. As the wood burns it heats the stones.
4. Rake the ash away. Beware: the coals will be hot, and sometimes the hot rocks underneath may explode!
5. Wrap the meat thoroughly in green or wet grass, or leaves.
6. Place the meat in the hot pit. You can leave the kangaroo's legs poking up out of the hole.
7. Pile earth into the hole.
8. Leave it for an hour if you're hungry, and don't mind bloody meat, four hours to get it well cooked, or all day or overnight if you're not in a hurry to eat it and like your meat warm and tender.

In the Kimberleys in northern Western Australia Aboriginal people filled the roo's stomach with liver and fat and blood and baked it like a sort of giant sausage in an earth oven. In some places they baked the whole animal in an earth oven. Earth ovens are still used today, and food cooked in them tastes wonderful.

Other times hunks of meat were cooked on a spit over the fire, or held over the fire on sticks, or wrapped in leaves and cooked in the hot ashes or hot coals of a fire. Often the roo was eaten half raw, still red and bloody.

The men prized the blood. They gathered it in bowls and shared it, or rubbed it on their spears or weapons.

Meat was always shared in Aboriginal communities. The kangaroo would be cut up by the hunter who had caught it. Usually the meat was divided according to law, though this varied from nation to nation, with each of the hunter's relatives getting a certain portion. Often the hunter might only get a small piece of meat, and had to rely on other people sharing their catch with him.

If you look at some traditional paintings of kangaroos, you'll see that the animal looks as though it's been divided up by a series of lines. These may match the traditional way the meat was supposed to be divided.

Kangaroos were used for much more than meat, too. Men and women chewed kangaroo sinew from the powerful back legs to make a strong and flexible

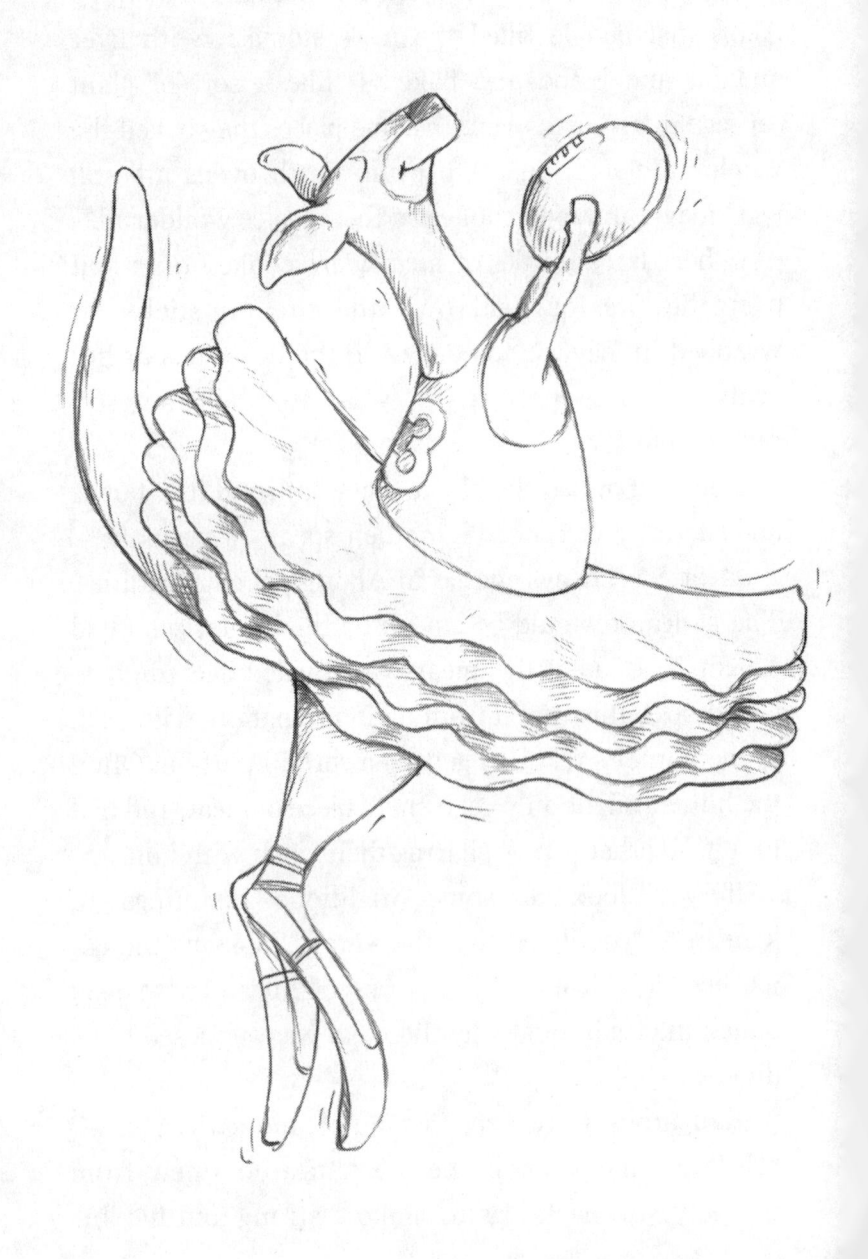

kind of string. The men used the string to fasten stone blades to axes, or spearheads to spears. As the fresh sinew dried it shrank, holding the quartz or other sharp rock tightly to the wooden handle.

The women used kangaroo leg sinew thread in kangaroo leg bone needles to sew kangaroo- or possum-skin cloaks. Possum skins were softer and much fluffier. If there were possums around no-one bothered much about kangaroo or wallaby cloaks.

Children and adults played ball games using balls made from kangaroo bladders or stomachs or other bits, filled with grass or leaves.

> **Fact**
>
> The Kurnai people of Victoria may have invented Australian Rules football. They played a leaping sort of football with a ball made of the scrotum of an 'old man' kangaroo, stuffed with grass.

People also made kangaroo-skin belts to hang their tools from, or used kangaroo skin to make handles for bags to collect fruit or yams or grass seeds, or as headbands to stop the sweat dripping into a hunter's eyes. In the area near present-day Gunning, near Canberra, only the bravest warriors could win the right to wear a kangaroo-skin bracelet on his arm.

How to make a kangaroo-skin rug or cloak

1. Catch your kangaroo — the fur of a young female one is softest.
2. Make a cut between the tendons of the back legs and thread through a rope made from woven grass or sinew. Now hang the roo from a branch in a tree.
3. Make a shallow cut in the skin around the neck and legs and pull the skin off — a bit like taking off a big, complicated glove.
4. Scrape off any fat, meat and sinew with your sharp stone or shell scraper.
5. Stretch the skin out flat by the fire until it dries. You'll need to arrange stones around the edges or it will curl up.
6. Rub it with wood ash while it's drying. This will keep the flies off, and also help keep it soft.
7. As soon as the skin is dry, rub in as much emu oil or goanna fat as you can, two or three times a day, to soften the skin.
8. Now ask a friend to help you pull the skin back and forth over the trunk of a smooth-barked tree until it's soft and pliable.
9. Trim the skin neatly then sew it to other skins to make a cloak or rug with thread made from the long tendons near the tail of the kangaroo.
10. You can wear your cloak when it's cold, or use it to carry tools from one camp to another.

But one thing was impossible with kangaroos — roos could never be trained to pull a cart or to be ridden or pull a plough. Horses, llamas, alpacas, yaks, oxen, water buffalo, ponies, cows and other animals (even goats and dogs) were tamed in the rest of the world to act as servants or partners for humans. But there were no animals, native to Australia, that could be domesticated. (You try riding a kangaroo. On second thoughts, don't. The kangaroo definitely wouldn't like it.)

How Europeans saw their first roos

The first written record of outsiders seeing roos comes from when the Dutch ship *Batavia* was sailing from Holland to Batavia (now Jakarta) and it was wrecked off Houtman Abrolhos, off the Western Australian coast in 1629.

The *Batavia*'s commander, François Pelsart, was one of the first Europeans to explore part of Australia, too — though he didn't really want to.

Pelsart was only trying to find water, as the stranded survivors were desperately thirsty. The only water he could find were rain puddles in the rocks. But he did find strange hopping creatures.

According to Pelsart the animals were about the size of a hare, with short front paws, and big back legs; they had a long tail and sat on their hind legs to eat. He thought that they were a weird kind of cat! But they were probably Tammar wallabies.

Pelsart decided that the young 'cats' were born in the mother's pouch, which isn't true, but he wasn't far wrong either (*see* Chapter 1).

Did the Chinese find roos?

There are rumours that a zoo in China had a kangaroo in the 1600s, though I haven't been able to find any proof. But some things, like fine stone weapons and axes and feathers, *were* traded right across Australia and up through southeast Asia long before white people arrived here. So it's quite possible that a weird animal like a kangaroo could end up in a Chinese zoo.

It's also very possible that Chinese explorers came down to Australia, and they might have taken some roos back. However, although we know China sent out explorers in the 1400s, there is no record of them coming here.

It's pretty likely other explorers had seen kangaroos or wallabies before Pelsart — especially Captain Abel Tasman in the early 1640s, who mapped over 3,000 kilometres of the northwestern coastline of Australia. But if Tasman saw roos he didn't think them worth mentioning. So Pelsart's is the first written record that we have.

The next person to write down an account of roos or wallabies was another Dutchman, Samuel Volkerson, in 1658. He described the Rottnest 'rats' on what's now Rottnest Island, also off the Western Australian coast. (We now know the 'rats' are tiny wallabies called Quokkas.) He also saw a 'wild cat', which was probably a Short-tailed Wallaby (*Setonix brachyurus*).

When the English pirate William Dampier was hunting for gold in Western Australia, he saw 'a sort of racoon' with short forelegs and long back legs that jumped around a lot. (He didn't find any gold though.) They were probably Banded Hare-wallabies (*Lagostrophus fasciatus*).

None of these accidental explorers was really interested in roos or wallabies — they wanted fresh water, or a safe harbour for their ships, or gold or spices. They didn't even bother to give the new creatures a name, until Englishman Captain James Cook decided to sail up the east coast of Australia.

How roos and wallabies got their names
Captain James Cook was the person who first called the big hopping animals 'kangaroos'.

In 1768, Cook was given command of a new expedition to the Pacific to search for *Terra Australis Incognita*, the mythical Great South Land. He wasn't heading for Australia, or 'New Holland' as it was called then, at all. New Holland had already been mapped on three sides by Dutch explorers, and they all agreed it was too hot, too poor, and too boring. It also didn't have good safe harbours for ships or fresh water to drink, and no rich gold or spices.

But as Cook's ship *Endeavour* sailed through the fierce storms in the Southern Ocean and off New Zealand, the small ship was battered and weakened. They were also running out of food. So Cook decided to head back up the unmapped east coast of Australia so that they could get back to Batavia (Java) quickly to repair his ship and get more supplies. On the way, they saw ... well, we're still not quite sure what animal Cook saw!

The first place that Cook sailed into along the Australian coast was a bay he called 'Sting-Ray Harbour', though he later changed its name to 'Botany Bay'. While the sailors searched for fresh water ashore, Captain Cook, botanists Sir Joseph Banks and Dr Solander, and seven other crew members went out to explore the land. They saw a 'quadruped' — a four legged animal — as big as a rabbit, which Banks's greyhounds almost caught. It might have been a small wombat, or a bandicoot. But it could have been a pademelon, which is a small wallaby.

However, they still didn't bother giving this weird new creature a name. It was only after the ship was wrecked at Endeavour Reef, off the coast of what now is Cooktown in north Queensland, that Cook and his crew spent enough time ashore (while they repaired the ship) to really study the local animals — and eat them too.

Cook sent a party out to shoot pigeons to make soup for sick crew members. The men saw a swift animal the size of a greyhound and the colour of a mouse. Cook saw the animal a few days later, too, and declared it was unlike any animal he had ever seen — hopping and jumping on its back legs and only using its front legs for scratching. He said that the local people called this strange creature a *kangaroo* or *kanguru*. There were plenty of these 'kanguru' around. Soon Cook and his crew were eating them, too.

But what *was* this mysterious animal that Cook saw? It wasn't the Grey or Red Kangaroo that we know today, because there weren't any up by the Endeavour River. And roos are too big to be the little animal that Cook saw. It was probably a Whiptail Wallaby.

But when the first settlers arrived at what's now Sydney, they saw a big animal that hopped. They assumed that it was the same kind that Cook saw at the top end of the continent. So they called it a 'kangaroo'. And that's how the Whiptail Wallaby — called kangaroo in the Guugu Yimithirr language — gave its name to the big Grey and Red Kangaroos that we know today.

Whiptail Wallaby

Or did it? According to some Guugu Yimithirr speakers *gunguru* means 'What did you say?' not 'small, hopping marsupial'. Maybe the person Cook spoke to was really trying to find out what this stranger was saying!

So what should kangaroos *really* be called? The trouble is there are just too many names to choose from. There were about 500 different languages in Australia when white settlers arrived, one for each of the many indigenous nations (just like there were many languages in Europe or Africa), and every one of them had a word for 'wallaby' or 'kangaroo'.

In the language of the Eora, the people of the Sydney region, the Eastern Grey Kangaroo is called *badagarang*. The Swamp Wallaby is *banggarai*.

The Wiradjuri people of central southern New South Wales called the kangaroo *bandharr*, *wambuuwayn*, *yuuluuma* or *ganuur*. Black Wallaroos were *walarro* (which is where our word 'wallaroo' comes from) and Rock Wallabies *barrbaay*.

The Nyungar people of what's now southwest Western Australia called the Tammar Wallaby *dhamar*, a baby kangaroo *dhudhiny*, and a kangaroo *yongkar*. The eastern Arrernte of Central Australia call Red Kangaroos *aheree* and Rock Wallabies *arrwe*.

It's much easier to understand how the wallaby got its name!

The Eora or indigenous people around what's now Sydney called a wallaby *wulaba*. The new settlers heard the word as 'wallaby', and that's what they called the small bounding animals that they saw.

What's in a name?

Australia's rugby union team is called the Wallabies, even though wallabies are small and the footballers are big. But they might have taken the name because the national rugby league team that toured Britain in 1908 had already claimed the name Kangaroos. The North Melbourne AFL club is called the Kangaroos. Maybe people like to call football teams after kangaroos and wallabies because footballers also leap into the air.

Roo stew and other colonial yum-yums

The first European settlers who arrived at what was to become Sydney *loved* to eat kangaroo. They mostly grilled them over the fire — there were few ovens. A great meal for a hungry settler was called Slippery Bob, a dish of battered kangaroo brains fried in emu fat.

The newcomers had guns; shooting rather than spearing made it much easier to hunt roos. Even some convicts were given guns to hunt kangaroos, as food was in short supply.

The newcomers were fascinated by the roos, too. Three years after the First Fleet landed a live kangaroo was sent to King George III of England, to show him what strange animals this new land had.

> **Fact**
>
> When the hungry convicts were given guns to hunt roos in the colony of Van Diemen's Land (later to become Tasmania) many of the convicts — and their guns — were never seen again. Known as the 'demons' of Van Diemen's Land, many became bushrangers and caused terror to new farmers and to the Aboriginal people for decades.

And in the first few decades as the first settlers explored their new country there seemed to be herds of roos everywhere. This was because the explorers mostly only explored the country along the rivers and coast, where there was plenty of grass for sheep and cattle to eat — and found roos already there munching on grass, too.

In fact, the roos kept the grass so short (as did the fire-stick farming) that areas like the Monaro and Tableland country in New South Wales looked like vast European parks, with animals grazing under the trees.

The new settlers continued eating kangaroo meat for decades. (Wallaby meat tasted too strong for most of them). Mostly the roo meat was roasted over a fire, as isolated shepherds didn't have stoves or cooking pots.

Sometimes the settlers only ate the kangaroo tails. They threw the tails onto a hot fire, skin and all, for half an hour. Then the charred tail was hauled off and the skin scraped away. The settlers ate the strong, tough meat with a hunk of damper, and treacle, if the ants hadn't got into it.

Wealthier households invented fancier kangaroo dishes. You could have roast kangaroo stuffed with suet, breadcrumbs, herbs and bacon, with a gravy made from milk and kangaroo stock and served with red currant jelly. Or perhaps you'd like kangaroo 'hash' for breakfast — cold slices of roast kangaroo heated up in last night's gravy, with a dash of port, lemon juice and tomato sauce.

A more modest household might eat kangaroo 'steamer'. Steamer was a good way to make tough meat tender. You put pieces of kangaroo in an iron pot with a heavy lid by a slow fire. The meat stewed in its own juices for hours, till it was tender. Sometimes onions were added or chopped bacon or pickled mushrooms or salted pork. There was kangaroo tail soup, too, which was dark brown and full of flavour, and eaten with bits of toast.

By the 1880s European settlers weren't eating so much kangaroo, as mutton was becoming cheap in the towns. Out in the bush it was easier to grab a sheep from the back paddock than go chasing kangaroos. There weren't as many roos left, either. Sheep and cattle now grazed the vast grasslands, and farmers believed that kangaroos 'stole' their grass. They shot roos and wallabies to feed their dogs, or sold the skins to make rugs or soft toys. Often they left the meat for the flies. And that's the way it stayed for nearly a hundred years.

How roos and some wallabies recovered

By the 1930s much of the roos' land had been taken for farms. So why were there more roos than ever before in some places? One reason was because there weren't as many dingoes left. Dingoes ate sheep as well as roos, so the farmers shot the dingoes. There were also fewer indigenous people hunting kangaroos.

But mostly the new settlers had become better farmers. In the early days of the colonies they just bunged on some sheep or cattle, got some convicts to make sure they didn't stray, and sold the young lambs and calves. But by the 1880s the grassy plains and bush were being fenced into paddocks with new fencing wire, and by the 1920s superphosphate was replacing some of the soil's plant food that had vanished into the tummies of sheep and cattle.

Farmers dug dams too. Now places that never had water before could support kangaroos, as well as sheep and cattle. Inland bores tapped into the Great Artesian Basin, the water deep below the Earth. Farmers planted new types of grasses that survived drought periods, or grew faster in winter, or were just better quality food — better tasting and more nutritious.

This was all supposed to be for the sheep and cattle of course, not for the kangaroos. But the roos happily drank the water and ate the new grass. And these happy, well-fed creatures had babies, and more babies . . .

There were still many areas where roos were wiped out, or almost wiped out, by farmers who didn't want kangaroos on their land, especially near towns and cities. But the roos' ability to breed fast and live on the same country area as sheep and cattle meant that in other places there were lots of roos. So they weren't in danger of all being killed and becoming extinct.

But things weren't as good for the wallabies. Kangaroos like open grasslands — just like sheep and cattle — so clearing the land for farming was good for them. But most wallabies need the shade of trees or rocks. They go blind if they get too much sunlight. In many places there just wasn't enough forest left for these smaller creatures.

By the 1920s Australians were finally starting to value their native animals, and their native plants and bushland, too. Many people were worried that too much land was being cleared and that too many native animals were being killed, and some species were vanishing forever. So what could we do?

Our first national park

The world's first national park, Yellowstone National Park, was established in the United States in 1872. But Australia wasn't far behind, with the world's second national park, Royal National Park near Sydney opening in 1879. And as years went by people lobbied governments for more parks to keep bushland for wild animals to live in, so that generations to come could enjoy them and so that the world didn't become one giant human suburb, with a few big farms for food. These parks are now the only home for many rare wallabies in Australia.

Boxing kangaroos

The Royal Australian Air Force No. 21 Squadron adopted the boxing kangaroo as its emblem in 1936. And the boxing kangaroo was painted on Australian planes in the Second World War. Alan Bond used it as his flag when his yacht won the America's Cup in 1983. It's now the emblem of the Australian Olympic team.

But the boxing kangaroo motif is much older than 1936. Travelling boxing teams in the 1800s displayed the boxing kangaroo on their tents. There was a 1936 movie about a boxing circus kangaroo too, and even an early bus company that used it as its emblem.

Today, all our native animals are protected. You need a permit to shoot any animals that may be threatening your crops.

But laws aren't much use if no-one makes sure that they are enforced. In most farming areas away from big towns police often don't know or care if a farmer shoots roos or wallabies — even endangered ones — on their own property. It's not difficult to acquire a permit to shoot kangaroos on your land, as long as you can put forward a case that they are a pest and that you have a gun licence. Lots of farm dogs still eat roos shot by their owners. Sadly, many shooters don't care about the difference between a kangaroo and a rare wallaby. Roos are also killed under licence by professional shooters though professional shooters mostly only kill roos that have bred into giant mobs — and they do know the difference between a roo and a rare wallaby.

We've come a long way since all kangaroos were hunted. But if roos, and especially wallabies, are to survive more people need to understand what they need and care about their preservation.

4

What roo is that?

Australia is a big place, and there are species of kangaroo or wallaby to suit every kind of country landscape — hot, dry, rocky, lush, sandy or mountainous. Some roos live in trees, some are furry giants — and some are tiny.

The smallest wallaby in the world is the Warabi Wallaby (*Petrogale burbidgei*). It's only about a metre long and weighs about a kilogram. It lives up in rugged and remote parts of the Kimberleys. Unfortunately, there aren't very many of them. No-one really knows how many are left, or much else about them.

The largest roo of all is the big Red Kangaroo (*Macropus rufus*). Big Reds can stand two metres tall and weigh around ninety kilograms. Sometimes mobs of 400 big Reds will bound across the desert, looking for grass or water during droughts.

About the only thing a big Red has in common with a Warabi is the big hind legs for jumping. But what about the Tree-kangaroo that can leap from branch to branch, or Quokkas . . .

There isn't room in this book to describe every roo or wallaby, but these are the most common, and the most amazing, ones.

The Eastern Grey — the most common roo

Most people only ever meet roos in the zoo. And the roo that is most likely to be in a zoo is the one which appears on Australia's coat of arms — the Eastern Grey Kangaroo (*Macropus giganteus*). Eastern Greys live in eastern Australia, throughout most of New South Wales, Victoria and the eastern half of Queensland — where most people live, too. So if you're bushwalking and see a roo, there's a good chance that it's an Eastern Grey. They usually live in forest country or grasslands — wherever there's more than about 250 millimitres of rain a year to grow the type of grass they need to eat.

An Eastern Grey is a tall, elegant-looking animal. It can grow nearly two-and-a-half-metres tall, and can weigh up to seventy kilograms. They are incredible jumpers, and the big ones can jump over a paddock fence without much noticing that it was there. But the young roos often get their legs caught as they try to jump over wire fences. Sometimes they break their foot (which means they can't jump and usually die), and other times they are trapped and die of thirst caught in the fence.

> ### Fact
>
> An Eastern Grey Kangaroo can not only jump over a one-and-a-half-metre fence; it can jump over a one-and-a-half-metre human!
>
> One day I was walking up one of our hills in a dream ... and met a big male Grey Kangaroo bounding down. I think he must have been daydreaming too, because suddenly we were face to face, about a metre away from each other. I jumped ... and he jumped too, right over me! For a second all I could see was a big, smelly roo bum ... And then he was gone.

Grey roos live in mobs. There's a big boss male roo, and several females and their joeys which belong to him. Sometimes several mobs will live together, with the males staying politely out of each other's way — unless they get too near 'their' females.

The big boss fights any other male in the mob who tries to be boss. He's the only one allowed to mate with all the females, and the younger males must stay out of his way.

Eastern Grey Kangaroo

Once a young male is about two years old he might decide to try to be boss instead. The two roos will fight it out. They'll box and try to rip each other with their hind claws and bite one another, sometimes badly injuring themselves. If the big old male loses the fight he might stay with the mob, keeping well out of the way of the new boss roo. Or he might become a solitary roo, and leave the mob to live by himself.

Could *you* box a kangaroo?

Definitely not, if you are a kid — and probably not even if you are a world champion boxer! I once watched two Eastern Grey males fight for three days and nights. By the third day they could hardly stand. One would aim a blow at the other, then they'd both pant for a minute or so to catch their breath, then the other would try to strike back. Finally, they were both so bushed that they both gave in and staggered away . . . and while the epic battle raged the females just ignored them and continued eating.

But are roos better boxers than humans? Well, humans probably know a lot more techniques because they have studied boxing. But a big roo can be taller and stronger than a human, and they also have claws on their toes to disembowel their enemies. So a roo might well win the fight.

Do not try it!

Sometimes young male roos go off and live with other young males rather than fight the boss roo of their mob. Then, when they are bigger and stronger, they may come back and try to win the mob for themselves. If the challenger wins he'll take over the females and become the new boss.

Eastern Greys generally live for about eight years, though they can live up to twenty years in very good conditions.

Eastern Grey Kangaroos, like most roos and wallabies, are awake from late afternoon to early morning, then during the heat of the day they rest in the shade of shrubs and trees. They do most of their feeding in the early evening or very early morning, though on moonlit nights you can see mobs munching on grass, too.

Eastern Greys mate in early summer, and the joey is born after thirty-six days. It begins poking its head out of the pouch at seven months old and starts leaving the pouch at around nine months. It leaves the pouch completely a month or two later, but will keep pushing its head into its mum's pouch for a few more months to feed, even if there is another baby there — and (unless conditions are particularly harsh) there usually is. But like all roos and wallabies the different-aged joeys each feed from a different teat (*see* Chapter 1).

As with other roos and wallabies, the Eastern Greys can breed very quickly, though, unlike some roos, the females can't get pregnant straight after a baby is born — the joey must be at least four months old, or even a few months older than this. But it still means that in good conditions a mob of roos can double in size in a year. And after a few good years there can be more Eastern Greys than the land can support.

A few hundred years ago this didn't matter, as the roos could just bound off to find new territory. But now the country is divided into farms and paddocks, and crossed by roads where roaming roos are killed by cars. Most grasslands now are kept for sheep and cattle. Eastern Greys aren't endangered, but the world they once owned has now vanished.

The Western Grey — a most smelly roo

The Western Grey Kangaroo (*Macropus fuliginosus*) is sometimes called a 'stinker'. The males in particular have a very strong smell of roo. (It's not a bad smell — just a strong one.) The pong lingers! In fact, if a mob of Western Greys has been around, you can still smell them a couple of hours later.

Western Greys are pretty similar to the Eastern Greys, though they're usually smaller and have more whiskers on their nose. But Greys generally vary a lot in size, and tend to grow bigger if there's good tucker around. So most people can't tell an Eastern Grey from a Western Grey.

Even though they are described as a Western Grey, their range extends east to include parts of Victoria, New South Wales and Queensland.

The big Red, the most muscular roo

You may not be able to tell an Eastern Grey from a Western one, but it's pretty easy to tell if you're looking at a big Red Kangaroo (*Macropus rufus*).

Big Reds are the world's biggest roo — we're talking muscle power! (Luckily, they don't have fangs like one of their ancestors!) The big Red's tail can be a metre long and strong enough to break your arm. It has a long squarish muzzle and very long ears that swivel round so it can catch the slightest noise — think horse's heads and you're in the right sort of field, more big and noble than pretty.

> **Fact**
> Actually the big Red Kangaroo usually isn't particularly red at all. The male is a sort of rusty colour, though in some areas of his coat he does look much brighter and redder. The female's coat is a soft bluish-grey (sometimes she is referred to as the 'blue flier'). You can tell a big Red female from a Grey Kangaroo by her white front and much chunkier face.

A big Red isn't usually quite as tall as the Grey, but it can weigh up to ninety kilograms — that's twenty kilograms more than a Grey. And those muscular shoulders and square noses just yell, 'Hey, I'm tough!'

Red Kangaroo

Big Reds need to be tough. They live over most of Australia — the driest, more westerly regions where few humans live, with an average rainfall of less than 500 millimetres a year. A big Red can nose out grass among the sand dunes or in rocky deserts, and if a waterhole dries up those giant legs can take them hundreds of kilometres across the harshest country to find new grass to graze.

If the grass is lush and green big Reds don't need to drink at all. But if the grass is brown and dry they drink from waterholes, or even scratch damp sand to find a seep of water underneath. Like many animals big Reds mostly drink at dusk or in the early morning. During the day they sleep in the shade of trees or boulders, so they do prefer country where there's shade for them to rest in during the day.

Just like the Greys, big Reds live in mobs, but they are *big*. There can be 400 roos in just one mob, though at other times there might just be the one, big dominant boss male, three or four adult females with maybe four or eight young roos living out of the pouch, and others still in the pouch.

The very big mobs may have many boss roos. They tactfully steer clear of each other, as long as another male doesn't sniff near 'their' females.

Female Red Kangaroos start breeding when they are fifteen months to two years old. If it's dry and there's not much grass or water they won't start breeding until it rains, so they can be three or even older when they have their first baby.

About half the babies born don't live to be adults. The baby stays in the pouch till it's seven or eight months old, but will stay close to its mum until it's about a year old, having a drink sometimes by sticking its head in her pouch. Big Reds live to about eight years old, though if conditions are good they may live longer, to about twenty, though this is very rare.

The Red-necked Wallaby — a roo, too

If you're in Tasmania the roo you're most likely to see will be what is also known as Bennett's Wallaby, though on the mainland it's called the Red-necked Wallaby (*Macropus rufogriseus*).

Red-necked Wallabies are one of the few wallabies that have done well from land clearing. They love areas with scattered trees, which offer them shelter during the day, and grassy areas instead of thick forest where they can feed from late afternoon to early morning, as well as dawn and dusk. This also means that it's easy to see them out in the open in cleared paddocks and next to roads, especially on late winter afternoons.

The Red-neck is smaller than a Grey and Red Kangaroo, being between seventy-seven to eighty-five centimetres long. It has a tail just slightly shorter than its body, with beautiful soft, fluffy fur, reddish on the shoulders and grey everywhere else. Red-necked Wallabies are common from southeast Queensland and the southern and eastern parts of Australia into eastern South Australia, down through Tasmania and the islands in Bass Strait.

Red-necks don't form mobs like the big kangaroos, so there's no boss roo. They like to feed on grassy flats near forest where often ten to thirty Red-necks will all be grazing together, but when they've finished feeding they'll all go their separate

Red-necked Wallaby

ways. During the day, they mostly sleep by themselves, usually under bushes or in the dense shade of trees. Red-necked Wallabies very quickly get used to humans or cars — which is bad for them, as they stop running away and shooters find them an easy target.

On the mainland Red-necks can breed at any time of year, but in Tasmania most are born in February and March, though they can be born anytime between January and July. Just about all female Red-necks that are old enough to breed will have babies in their pouch.

> **Fact**
>
> The Red-necked Wallaby used to be shot for its long, soft fur. The skin was mostly made into rugs, but these days this wallaby is protected.

The Swamp Wallaby — the worst manners

I love Swampies (*Wallabia bicolor*), which are also known as the Black-tailed Wallaby, Black Wallaby, Stinkers and Fern Wallaby. Okay, so they eat my roses, guzzle my garden, trample down my bulbs, squeeze holes in my fences and totally ignore me if I try to shoo them away. They're not delicate or graceful like other wallabies either, and their table manners are revolting. (You should see one munching through an orange, with all the sticky juice running down its tummy, or sucking down wonga vine like it was spaghetti).

Swampies have coarse, dull grey to dark brown or black and reddish fur. This is lucky for them, because it means that they have never been hunted for their fur, especially by the Aboriginal people, who would prefer to use soft fur wherever possible. Their meat tastes quite strong too — and sometimes foul — so most Aboriginal people didn't bother eating them much, either.

But I've spent most of my life around Swampies now, and I've finally got to the stage where I can watch a mother Swampy pull down a branch of my roses for the baby in her pouch to eat, and think, 'Hey, sweet,' instead of 'Get out of it, you furry thief!'

The Swampy is the only *true* wallaby, that is, it is the only one whose scientific name is *Wallabia*. And it looks like a classic wallaby, too, with narrow shoulders instead of muscular ones like a roo, a rounded back and a small head. Swampies don't bound for kilometres like roos, either. Mostly, they just lope about a bit, looking for food — or jump to the next bit of bush to hide in if they are startled.

The Swampy is about sixty-five to seventy-five centimetres long, with a tail about the same length as its body. It usually weighs somewhere between twelve to twenty kilograms. A Swampy is basically black on top, greyish on the sides and a rusty colour

Swamp Wallaby

underneath, with a paler face and dark areas around its eyes. But even in our valley Swampies vary a lot in colour. Some have white tips on their tails. Some are mostly black, and others have more reddish fur on their tummies, and some have lighter fawn faces. There are four sub-species of Swampy in Queensland, too, and they also vary a bit in colour.

Male Swampies are taller and much more muscular than the females, and far more boisterous, too. I can always tell when Rosie's new baby is a male. By the time it's about ten months old it has a muscly chest, and starts to box her or thump her in the tummy with its hind legs if she doesn't pull down the best branches for him to chew. (Rosie, on the other hand just calmly hops away and refuses to pull down any branches for the obstreperous baby until it starts to behave!)

Swampies are one of the most common and widespread wallabies, so you're most likely to see this wallaby than any other variety. Swampies live in the eastern parts of Australia, from the tip of Cape York right down to the southern coast of Victoria and there are still a few in the southern corner of South Australia.

In fact, Swampies can survive wherever there are plenty of young shrubs, grasses and leaves for them to munch on (including exotic varieties like pine trees), and especially plenty of nice shady shrubs and trees for them to shelter under during the day.

Those Swampies exposed to too much sunlight will go blind — their eyes turn pale and milky, rather than black. A blind Swampy can survive for years if it's in an area that it knows well, and which has plenty of food. But if a blind Swampy is attacked by a dog it won't be able to escape.

The story of Harry

Harry was an old wallaby when I first met him. I woke up one morning and there he was, outside the shed, nosing along the fence for some grass then sniffing higher and reaching up to grab some clematis leaves. Actually, Harry had probably been living near the shed most of his life. I just hadn't seen him before.

Young and fit wallabies, especially strong males, get the favourite feeding times, in the early morning and early evening. Other younger and weaker wallabies get the 'dark of the night' feeding times.

But Harry was old. He was forced to feed during the day when the other wallabies were asleep. And Harry was blind.

It was easy to see that he was blind, because both his eyes were milky, not dark. And as I watched him I could see that he sniffed his way around, instead of looking where he was going.

But Harry could still find his way around the garden by the shed, especially when it came to his favourite foods. A wallaby's sense of smell is not as good as that of a wombat, but it still relies on it a great deal. A wallaby will follow the scent of a wombat, too — it knows that a wombat is strong and can push its way through bushes, making a 'wombat path', or push or dig under a fence. So if the wallaby follows a wombat's scent, it can make use of the wombat's muscles.

'Hello,' I said.

Harry stopped munching clematis leaves and sniffed my way. He must have recognised my scent and known I wasn't a threat. He went back to eating.

I saw him every day after that. He'd be there when I got up, munching away. Then about lunchtime he'd slowly hop into the shade of a passionfruit vine.

The other wallabies who lived by the shed picked my oranges and apricots and lemons. But Harry mostly ate grass and vine leaves. I suppose it was too hard to find his way among the branches.

One day I heard barking up on the hill. By the time I'd run outside the dogs had found Harry. They were kelpies, black-and-white with shiny coats.

Harry panicked. He tried to run. But it's hard to run when you can't see. Within two leaps he had trapped himself against the fence.

He ran again. This time he landed against the vegie garden fence, struggling and catching his tail in the wire.

The dogs were nearly on him. I ran at them, yelling. But when dogs have the scent of the chase they don't stop.

I dashed in front of them, shielding Harry with my body. I don't think I'd do that now — when dogs hunt sometimes their wolf side takes over. Even loving pet dogs can savage you if you're between them and the animal they want.

But I was lucky.

'Down!' I yelled.

One dog hesitated, then sat. The other one glanced at him.

'Down! Sit!' I yelled again. 'No!'

The second dog dropped onto his tummy and rolled over. I grabbed him by his collar and hauled him over to the shed. The other followed.

I glanced back. Harry just stood there. He was shaking. He didn't move even when I took the dogs indoors.

The dogs sat as I gave them bowls of water — which they didn't want. I offered them some bread (I didn't have any meat). They ate it ravenously, so I gave them some more, and more after that. Then I rang the number on their collars.

Yes, I had been lucky. So had Harry. The dogs were lost; they'd run off into the bush when their owner had 'let them out for a run' on their way down to the coast. They were lost and unhappy. They wanted a human to look after them and tell them what to do. They'd been much more interested in me than in Harry.

I tied some string around their collars and led them out to the car to take them up to town to wait for their owner to pick them up.

Harry still hadn't moved. He was in shock, still trembling. But there wasn't anything I could do to help him. If I'd approached him I'd have scared him even more. He was still there when I got back home.

The next morning he was gone. I hunted around the shed and finally found him, down at the end of the garden, munching his grass as though nothing had happened — though he did sniff more warily when I came near. Maybe the smell of dog lingered, or maybe he was just making sure I was alone.

Harry stayed grazing around the shed for another two years. His coat grew greyer. He hopped more slowly too, and seemed to sleep for longer.

Then one day he wasn't there at all. I found him down by the creek, by the path he always used to go to the water. I didn't bury him — the ground was too hard and dry to dig that summer. Besides, he was a wild animal. He belonged to the other wild animals he lived with — the goannas, who eat the carcases, the crows, the eagles. Within a couple of days he was gone.

Swampies are nocturnal — they graze at night, especially at dusk and in the early morning before it gets too light. But old or blind wallabies will graze during the day. Mostly Swampies only drink in the early evening, then again in the early morning before they head off to dense shade to sleep during the heat and brightness of the day. But on very hot days, especially if the grass or leaves they've been eating have been dryish, they'll hop to a pool or creek for an extra drink.

Unlike kangaroos and many other wallabies, Swampies don't travel much. They like staying in their own territory, though several Swamp Wallabies may share the same territory, on a sort of 'time share' basis. Some feed there at some times, and others at other times.

Mostly Swampies live by themselves, not in a mob. But a mother wallaby may have a baby in her pouch and a couple of her older joeys still with her much of the time.

The area of a Swamp Wallaby's territory depends on how much food is about. Around my place it can range from about half a hectare in our garden, with lots of roses and carrots to pinch, to about ten hectares up on the hills where there isn't so much for wallabies to eat.

But sometimes we have eleven Swampies munching on our garden at the same time. (When you go outside at night the garden seems to jump away.) The Swampies keep tactfully away from each other.

Fact

A Swampy is a good jumper. It can leap twice its own height. And it can bound up an almost vertical slope, or down it too, where you or I would just fall down it.

Swampies hide if there's danger, staying very, very still. But they never seem to realise that even if they can't see you, you might still be able to see them. These wallabies often try to hide with their heads in a bush, or behind a fence, leaving their long black tails spread out like a fat, furry snake.

You may think Swampies aren't very bright. You'd be right.

Swampies breed all year round. Some only have two or three babies in their lives. Others, like Rosie, have a baby in their pouch all the time and one still sticking its head in the pouch to drink, and another 'teenager' keeping close to mum until it's about eighteen months old. Like other roos and wallabies, Swampies have four teats, all producing different milk for their joeys of different ages — and with Swampies at least three of these teats will be pretty much always in use. I've never known Rosie to not have a baby in her pouch.

> **Fact**
>
> You often see a Swampy with a bald spot on the top of its tail near its bottom. This is from wriggling under fences — as it crawls out the other side the Swampy's tail scrapes against the wire, slowly wearing off the hair.

Swampies are true gourmets — they think a diet of grass is boring! This also means that they are very good at finding food that they've never tried before. In very dry seasons here, when there hasn't been any grass for months, Rosie picks up fallen apples or avocadoes to pass to her baby — and tiny paws stretch out from her pouch to take the fruit.

Mostly Rosie isn't very interested in grass. But if there hasn't been any for months and then it rains again, Rosie changes her mind and munches away at the new lushness. She bends down right close to the ground as she eats — so low that the tiny baby in her pouch can eat the grass too. A Swampy joey starts to eat grass when it's so tiny — no bigger than a mouse, with hardly any fur — as it sticks its head out of mum's pouch.

Over the years I've discovered lots of plants that Swamp Wallabies don't eat (most of the time, anyway). But in very dry years, these wallabies eat many things they otherwise would ignore in good times — and survive. From rhubarb leaves to young avocado trees — if it's green they'll eat it. But when the good times come and the rain falls again, they return to eating what they like best.

Swampies use their hands more than any other wallaby. They can pick fruit from a tree with their paws, and even peel it delicately, though some Swampies like to eat the fruit skin and all. They use their paws to pull down branches, to hold apples while they nibble them, and to scratch themselves, too.

Fact

In some places, though not where I live, Swampies have been seen to eat meat. Meat in their diet is said to make them pong so badly that they've been known as 'stinkers'. (Our Swampies don't pong at all.) Well, sometimes they smell like old apricots especially when they've spent a few weeks guzzling all the fruit under the apricot trees.

The story of breakfast with Rosie

Rosie was outside the bedroom window when I woke up one morning, eating an apple she'd just picked from the tree. I could hear the crunch, crunch, crunch as she munched it.

I peered out the window just as an even smaller pair of paws reached up from Rosie's pouch and snatched the apple. Instead of 'crunch, crunch, crunch', I could hear 'snibble, snibble, snibble' as Rosie's baby began to eat the apple instead. But Rosie is a patient mum. She just reached up and picked another apple for herself.

Rosie is dedicated to her babies. She always has one in her pouch, one half-grown one bounding along beside her, sometimes pushing its head back into the pouch for a drink, and another almost grown-up joey who still likes to hang around mum — and sometimes have a drink as well.

The only time I've ever seen Rosie lose her patience with a joey was last year, when she was using one paw to pull down a branch of rose leaves to eat herself, and holding another branch in the other paw so that baby Fuzz-face could eat as well. Except Fuzz decided that he wanted to eat Mum's roses instead. He reached up to grab the branch.

*Rosie loves to eat . . . roses
(and apples, lemons and asparagus, too)*

Rosie stood on tiptoe and held the branch up higher so Fuzz couldn't reach it.

Fuzz somersaulted out of the pouch. He *also* reached up on tiptoe to snatch the branch from his Mum's paws.

Rosie held the branch up even higher.

Fuzz grabbed his mum round the neck and kicked her in the tummy with both big feet . . .

Rosie let go of her branch — it's hard to keep eating roses while your joey is kicking you in the tummy. She waited calmly till Fuzz finished kicking . . . then slowly hopped away to another rose bush. She didn't even look back to see if Fuzz was following.

But this time when she pulled down a branch of roses she didn't haul one down for Fuzz, too.

Fuzz spent three days eating boring old grass, and trying to stand on tiptoe to reach the roses and the apples and the lemons and the cherry leaves and all the other good things his mum had hauled down for him before. At last he got the message. Be nice to Mum, mate, or you don't get good things to eat.

On the third day when I looked out the window, there they were again. Rosie had a rose in her mouth, and Fuzz had a rose in *his* mouth.

And this time Fuzz was very, very polite indeed.

The Tree-kangaroo — a most amazing roo

Kangaroos and wallabies usually jump around on the ground — they don't live in trees. Unless of course they're a Tree-kangaroo. There are only two species of Tree-kangaroo in Australia: Lumholtz's Tree-kangaroo (*Dendrolagus lumholtzi*) and Bennett's Tree-kangaroo (*Dendrolagus bennettianus*). The others all live in New Guinea.

> **Fact**
>
> Up until about 8,000 years ago Australia and New Guinea were all one country, known as the continent of Sahul. Then the glaciers of the last Ice Age melted, and the sea level rose. That's why northern Australia and New Guinea share some of their animals and plants.

Lumholtz's Tree-kangaroo lives in small patches of the Queensland rainforest on the Atherton Tablelands and surrounding hills. The local people called Lumholtz's Tree-kangaroo *boongarry*. Bennett's Tree-kangaroo lives in north Queensland too, between the Daintree and Cooktown. The local people called it *jarabeena*. Both species of Tree-kangaroo look and behave pretty much alike, though experts can tell the difference.

Lumholtz's Tree-kangaroo is about forty-eight to fifty-nine centimetres long. Its tail is longer than its body, and the animal weighs between three to seven kilograms. It is sooty-coloured on top, with a pale tummy and arms. It has a black face with a pale band across its forehead and down each side and on both hands and feet.

Bennett's Tree-kangaroo is browner, and is fifty to sixty-five centimetres long, and its tail is much longer than its body and, unlike Lumholtz's Tree-kangaroo, it has a black end to its tail. It also doesn't have a pale band on its face.

Unlike other roos and wallabies, which use their tails for balance and to travel along the ground, Tree-kangaroos use their tails to help them steady themselves as they move about from branch to branch. When they're sitting still their tails flop and hang down — they don't stand up in a curve or stick out stiffly.

The feet of Tree-kangaroos are shorter, too, with a rough sole to help them get a better grip on the trees. They are the only roos that can move one hind foot at a time while on land, as well as reach above their heads with their front paws. This helps them hold on to branches as they move about the trees.

Like the Swampies, Tree-kangaroos can hold food in their paws, or grip branches and vines. Actually, they can only move by gripping the branches with their front and back legs and running slowly along the branch. They can even go backwards. Sometimes

Tree-kangaroos can even hop on very level straight branches, much like roos hop on the ground.

When a Tree-kangaroo wants to come down from a tree it goes tail first, holding on to the tree with its front paws and sort of sliding with its back legs. Then when it's about two metres from the ground it lets go, and kicks the tree with its back legs, giving a massive leap onto the ground.

> **Fact**
>
> Whenever a Tree-kangaroo is startled or scared it can jump as much as fifteen metres down to the ground! This great leap means it can run — or hop — away very quickly once it's out of the tree. Unfortunately, it doesn't bound as well as other kangaroos. Instead, it gives a sort of hop on all fours, or a running shuffly hop on its hind legs.

Tree-kangaroos are nocturnal. They spend their days sitting in a tree fork or on a branch snoozing, and their nights eating or moving around looking for food. They usually stay among the treetops, but do come to ground when they want to go to another tree that's too far away to jump to.

Lumholtz's Tree-kangaroos mostly live by themselves. If two male Tree-kangaroos of this species meet they growl at each other, until one moves away. Sometimes they fight each other

Tree-kangaroo

viciously, especially if there is a female nearby. Females can have babies at any time of the year.

Bennett's Tree-kangaroos sometimes live in family groups. The males growl at each other and the females 'talk' to their joeys with a soft, hooshing, trumpeting sound. They feed on rainforest leaves, tree shoots and fruit. Bennett's Tree-kangaroo has been seen coming down to feed in people's vegie gardens, munching on corn and other vegies.

> **Fact**
>
> Lumholtz's Tree-kangaroo has the biggest tummy for its size of any roo. Its food is mostly coarse leaves, and its big tum allows time for the leaves to be digested.

Tree-kangaroos are so amazing that there are now special tours to see them in the wild, though sometimes you have to be lucky to see one.

Sadly, these days a lot of the habitat of the Tree-kangaroo has been cleared for logging, or for tourism to build holiday homes. Both species of Tree-kangaroo are now endangered. They'll need a lot of luck and support from people working to preserve the trees and land they live in if they are going to survive. It's sad to think these amazing creatures might be wiped out accidentally, by people clearing just one more bit of bush . . .

The Quokka — the cutest roo of all!

The Quokka (*Setonix branchyurus*) not only has the cutest name of any animal, it's one of the cutest marsupials, too. Even though there aren't very many Quokkas in the world, it's pretty easy to see them if you're determined — just take a trip out to Rottnest Island in Western Australia.

Samuel Volkertzoon, a Dutch sailor, was the first European who wrote about Quokkas. He thought they were tiny cats. Willem de Vlamingh, a Dutch navigator, thought they were rats. In 1696 he named the island off the Swan River in Western Australia, 'Rotte Nest' or 'Rat's Nest' Island after the little furry creatures.

But the indigenous people living in the Augusta and King George Sound area of southwest Western Australia called these cute little hoppers *Quokkas* — and that's the name we use now.

A Quokka is tiny. It's about eighty centimetres long and weighs around three or four kilograms. They have long, coarse grey fur.

As well as being smaller (and cuter) than most other wallabies, the Quokka also has a short, stiff tail — unlike the long flexible tail of other wallabies — and short hind feet. In fact, the Quokka has the shortest feet of any roo or wallaby. It's not so much a 'macro' pod as a 'micro' pod! It moves in a sort of rapid hop and leap, rather than the bounds and lopes of a wallaby. Its ears are more rounded, too, and its skull and teeth are different.

> **Fact**
>
> Quokkas spend most of their time on the ground, but they can also climb trees and have been seen up to two metres off the ground.

Before white settlers came there were plenty of Quokkas, both on Rottnest Island and across southwest Western Australia. But these days there are only small groups on the mainland, and lots on Rottnest Island, where feral cats and dogs can't attack them. There may be between 4,000 and 17,000 Quokkas on the island — the numbers vary a lot depending on whether the island has had good rain or not. Rain means food and water to drink.

Though Quakkas on Rottnest Island may be safe from cats and dogs, it's a harsh and often dry place for them to live. The Quokkas are usually okay in winter, which is when Rottnest Island gets most of its rain. It's also cooler and there's more lush grass and pigface, with its moist sappy leaves, though Quokkas can also strip the leaves and bark from small shrubs and eat just about any plant around. As long as their food is nice and soft and moist Quokkas can survive without drinking.

Unfortunately during summer life gets harder, especially in drought years. As the island becomes

Quokka

drier and hotter, and the plants dry out, the tiny animals travel up to two kilometres just to get near the freshwater soaks on the island. But each soak is 'owned' by the local Quokka mob of anywhere from twenty-five to 250 adults. The local males fight other Quokkas that try to come too close to the soaks or want to rest in their precious shade on hot days. Quokkas sleep during the day, but they need to shelter from the sunlight to survive.

Even though Quokkas can survive for long periods without drinking water, and have even been seen drinking salt water, many Quokkas become ill in summer when their island is dry. Quokkas that live far away from the water soaks die from a blood disorder called anaemia caused by lack of water and nitrogen in the dried out plants in summer.

> **Fact**
>
> Quokkas have been used by medical researchers to study muscular dystrophy as, like humans, they suffer from the same disease.

There are other problems for Quokkas on Rottnest Island, too. The island soils don't have much copper and cobalt, so the plants that grow there don't have high levels of these important minerals. Quokkas need copper and cobalt to breed successfully. Tourists sometimes try to feed Quokkas too — and human food like bread, chips and meat can make Quokkas very ill.

On Rottnest Island and Bald Island Quokkas mate between January and March. A single joey is born twenty-five to twenty-eight days later, towards the end of summer or in autumn. This is when the days are milder and there is more food and moisture, so the mother can provide milk for her baby.

On the mainland though, where there's better food, water and shade, the Quokkas can have a baby at any time of year. The baby joey stays in the pouch for about six months, but like other joeys will feed from its mum for longer; in the Quokka's case it's about four months.

The Rock Wallabies — rare endangered species

Roos and wallabies have been able to adapt to the harshest climate change on Earth, including the last Ice Age. They survived the land drying up, using their ability to cope on little water and their strong legs to travel long distances to find more food and water.

The one thing that many of these animals can't survive is humans.

Most kangaroos have done pretty well — in the past 200 years we've cleared land for farming, which is great for roos who likes grass and open spaces. But for wallabies who need shelter from the sun and shrubs to browse on, the outlook is not good. Humans now use most of Australia's water not just taking it from rivers but drilling bores so that springs and soaks in the bush dry up and animals die of thirst. And we've introduced feral animals, like goats, deer, pigs and foxes. (White settlers introduced foxes to Australia in the 1800s, so they could be hunted for sport. But the hunters weren't good enough to catch all the foxes that bred and spread throughout mainland Australia in all but the most arid regions.)

We've seen earlier how Tree-kangaroos and the Quokka are threatened, but one of the most vulnerable groups in Australia are Rock Wallabies. And that's because these wallabies need their rocks!

Rocky hills, rocky gorges, and rocky mountains — as long as Rock Wallabies have rocks to shelter among when it's hot, and interesting things to eat growing out of the rocks, and a spring or creek to drink from, then they are happy.

The trouble is that most rocky places are surrounded by areas that aren't rocky at all. So Rock Wallabies may be restricted to a very small area. And once their area is surrounded by humans or sheep or cattle they can't easily travel from one rocky area to another to mate. All too often there just aren't enough Rock Wallabies left to breed in that area, so the species dies out in that region. Rock wallabies are hunted by feral dogs too.

In many areas feral goats eat the Rock Wallabies' food. Goats can roam over grasslands once the food among the rocks has gone. But the Rock Wallabies can't, and so they starve. Rock Wallabies also die from toxoplasmosis, a disease spread by feral cats. Foxes are a big problem for Rock Wallabies, too. Rock Wallabies leave their joeys in a sheltered spot while they go out to drink or graze and foxes can squeeze into crevices where the babies shelter while their mothers are feeding.

Rock Wallabies don't *look* rare, either. They look pretty much like other wallabies, at least to shooters. We used to have Brush-tailed Rock Wallabies living in the steep cliffs around our place. But hunters would come down the mountain looking for roos for 'dog tucker'. The roos would run when they heard the men and dogs. But the Rock Wallabies would try to hide among the rocks — or be too sleepy to realise their danger till it was too late. The dogs would sniff them out...

I don't know if the last Rock Wallabies around here were shot, or killed by dogs, or just died of old age. If there are only a few animals they may not have healthy babies when they mate. (Often when animal populations are stressed there are a lot more male babies than female, and that means they're more likely to die out, too.)

Just about all Rock Wallaby species are threatened or endangered. Some of the rarest live in remote areas in northern Australia. And one of those is the smallest wallaby of all.

This is the Warabi Wallaby (*Petrogale burbidgei*). The Warabi is only about a metre long and weighs about a kilogram. It lives up in rugged and remote parts of the Kimberleys and was only described late last century. Not much is known about it.

Until the Warabi was found scientists thought the Nabarlek (*Petrogale concinna*) was the smallest. It is a Rock Wallaby too, and also lives high up in Arnhem Land and the Kimberleys.

The Nabarlek is the only marsupial that can grow more than the normal four molar teeth. Most of the native grasses the Nabarlek eats are particularly high in silica (which grinds teeth down) and this may explain why Nabarleks need to keep replacing their grinding (molar) teeth.

Warabi Wallaby

Nabarleks rest in caves and rock shelters during the day in the dry season, coming out at night to graze. But during the wet season Nabarleks feed during the afternoon as well, and often sleep on ledges out in the sun in the mornings. During the day Nabarleks have to be wary of sea eagles, great birds which swoop down and carry tiny Nabarleks away.

Another very rare and remote wallaby is the Black-footed Rock Wallaby (*Petrogale lateralis*), called *waru* in Western Desert Aboriginal languages. The *waru* used to live in many central desert regions of the Northern Territory, South Australia and Western

Australia. Now, there are only a few Black-footed Rock Wallabies left.

Herbert's Rock Wallaby (*Petrogale herberti*) is nearly as small as the Nabarlek, and only weighs about six kilograms or less. It has an incredibly bushy tail about fifty-five centimetres long that helps it to balance as it leaps across rocks. Herbert's Rock Wallabies are found in southeast Queensland.

The Proserpine Rock Wallaby (*Petrogale persephone*) is a shy and delicate-looking wallaby. Scientists only realised it was a separate species of wallaby in 1976. It lives in northeast coastal Queensland.

The Yellow-footed Rock Wallaby (*Petrogale xanthopus*) is probably the most beautifully coloured of all marsupials. It was hunted for its fur, and its skin was made into soft toys, coats and slippers. There used to be a lot of Yellow-footed Rock Wallabies throughout arid and semi-arid Australia, but these days they only survive in a few isolated rocky outcrops in New South Wales, South Australia and Queensland.

The most widespread Rock Wallaby these days is the Brush-tailed Rock Wallaby (*Petrogale penicillata*), though they too only live in a few places in New South Wales and Queensland and are an endangered species in New South Wales and Victoria.

All Rock Wallabies look slightly different from other wallabies. Their tail is thicker and less

Rock Wallaby

tapered, and can be carried arched over their back rather than flat out behind them. (A good solid tail is essential for balancing as they leap from rock to rock.)

Rock Wallabies live in groups of between ten to a hundred, though in areas where there aren't very many they may live by themselves, or with just two or three others. Their favourite places are rocky ledges where they can sit in the early mornings and late afternoons, and small caves in which to shelter during the heat of the day, with narrow crevices to leave their babies safe while they are out grazing. They mostly eat in the very early morning, or late afternoon or evening. In mid-summer the wallabies only eat late at night when it's cooler. Their main diet is grass, but they also eat leaves and new shoots and small plants.

Fact

Rock Wallabies love fruit too. We had a mob that loved apricots so much we called them 'the apricot guts wallabies'. Every Christmas in the late afternoon after the sun dropped below the ridge they'd bound down to the orchards and eat so many apricots that their tummies would bulge and they'd finally hop, very slowly, back up the hill to their rocks.

Rock Wallabies are amazing jumpers. They don't leap as high as many other roos and wallabies, but they are the most sure-footed leapers you can imagine. Even more amazing is the way they leap down slopes that are almost vertical. Somehow they manage to keep their footing and not fall down face first into the gorge below.

They leap from rock to rock too, as though they have springs on their feet. And unlike all other wallabies and roos, except for Tree-kangaroos and Quokkas, they can even climb trees, as long as the trees slope a bit. They don't cling on, like Tree-kangaroos, but just jump from branch to branch or fork to fork, somehow finding footholds as they go up the tree.

> **Fact**
>
> The soles of the feet of a Rock Wallaby are slightly rough, to help it get a better grip. (You try leaping up a nearly vertical rock face without slipping!)

If you think you may have come across a colony of Rock Wallabies, don't disturb them or go any closer. Just pick up some of their droppings. (They don't smell and they're not soft and squishy, either. Look for cylindrical droppings that are tapered at one end — rabbit and goat droppings are more rounded.) Then call the local national park ranger to ask where you can send them to be identified. The more we know about where endangered species live, the more can be done to protect and keep them safe.

And if you're out bushwalking near rocky outcrops, do keep an eye out for wallaby droppings, too. The Rock Wallaby is one of the shyest of all wallabies, and very good at hiding. So it's just possible that you may find a lost colony that no-one else knows about.

Amazing lost wallaby colonies

Over the years several lost wallaby colonies *have* been found!

One of these is the Nailtail Wallaby (*Onychogalea* species). There were once three species of Nailtail Wallabies. The Crescent Nailtail Wallaby (*Onychogalea lunata*) is extinct, and the Northern Nailtail (*Onychogalea urguifera*) is found across the top end of Australia and is still common. For a long time everyone thought the Bridled Nailtail Wallaby (*Onychogalea fraenata*) was extinct too, as no-one had seen one since 1937.

Then, in 1973, an article about Australia's extinct species appeared in a magazine and a fencing contractor reported that there was a population of Bridled Nailtail Wallabies on a property in central Queensland near the town of Dingo. The property eventually became Taunton National Park (Scientific).

In 1996, Bridled Nailtails were introduced to Idalia National Park, and there are now over 300 wallabies there. There are also about 100 wallabies on a farm reserve south of Emerald, Queensland.

> **Fact**
>
> Nailtails got their name because of the three-millimetre horny spur they have at the end of their tails. No-one knows why they have it, but it may act as a 'pivot' to help them turn or take off quickly. Nailtails used to be called 'flashjacks' because of their sudden bursts of speed.

Extinct wallabies that aren't!

Here's a riddle. The mainland Tammars are extinct — but there are thousands of them alive! How come? Well, it's a long story . . .

The tiny Tammar Wallaby (*Macropus eugenii*), with its cute short arms, rounded ears and short, sweet furry face, used to bound over large parts of southern and southwestern Australia.

But being 'little' and 'cute' also meant that these wallabies were small enough for foxes and even big feral cats to hunt them. So much of their land has been cleared that the mainland South Australian Tammar Wallaby is probably extinct.

> **Fact**
>
> The Tammar Wallaby takes its name from the *tammar* (the local word for the she-oak or casuarina tree) thickets where they lived in Western Australia.

Luckily, Tammars are still common on some Australian islands, like Kangaroo Island, where there are no foxes. These island Tammars have been separated from the mainland wallabies for 10,000 years, ever since the last Ice Age glaciers melted and Kangaroo Island became an island as the seas rose. In that time the island wallabies have evolved to become somewhat different from those on the mainland, so much so that they're now designated as several 'sub-species'. Tammars that used to live on Flinders Island, for example, were more graceful than the Kangaroo Island Tammars, and had shorter, finer fur. (Feral cats on Flinders Island may have killed the last of the Tammars living there.)

Then the mainland Tammars were discovered again... but not on the mainland!

In 1841, Sir George Grey was Governor of South Australia. He was appointed Governor of New Zealand in 1845, and then Governor of Cape Colony and High Commissioner for South Africa in 1854. But then in 1862 he was made Governor of New Zealand again, so Sir George bought Kawau Island, near Auckland, to live on. Sir George decided to bring animals from everywhere he'd lived to his island.

So ships brought him zebras, antelopes, kookaburras, Brush-tailed Rock Wallabies, Parma Wallabies, Swampies — and of course they brought the Tammar Wallabies. But where had Sir George found his Tammars? Did they come from one of the islands? Or, just possibly, were his Tammars from the mainland? Could Sir George have accidentally saved mainland Tammars from extinction? He had! And the wallabies continued to breed on the island off Auckland.

Finally, long after the Tammars had been taken from their home, eighty-five were brought back to South Australia in 2003 to 2004. In November 2004, ten radio-collared Tammar Wallabies (two males and eight females) were released in Innes National Park. But by February 2005, four had been killed by foxes.

In April 2005, a female Tammar (with a joey in its pouch) was killed when she was hit by a car. And in May 2005, one male wallaby died, too. Which left only four of the ten still alive. But three of those had joeys in 2005 and 2006.

In June 2005, another thirty-six wallabies were released. But eighteen died in the next two months, probably from starvation — the food in the national park was just too strange for them.

Since then the speed limit has been reduced in the park, so that speeding drivers hopefully won't hit wallabies. Foxes have been baited and food left out for the wallabies.

Will the Tammars survive? They've got a good chance. Even though so many of the released wallabies have died, the ones that have survived are having babies — and the babies look like they've learned how to keep surviving in the national park. More Tammars are being bred at Monarto Zoological Gardens too, and some have been released down on Yorke Peninsula.

Tammars like nice thick bushes to shelter under away from the heat and also where they can hide from predators and hunters. But they also like open grassy areas where they can feed, as they mostly eat grass, though if there isn't much grass they'll eat leaves and weeds too.

Tammars have their own territory, but other Tammars usually live there as well. Though they don't live in mobs they are sweet-natured little wallabies, who don't mind sharing their living space.

Tammar Wallabies have a really astounding way of breeding. The mothers mate at different times, but then all the fertilised eggs just stay dormant inside the mother until the summer solstice — the longest days of the year, the 22 and 23 December — when all the foetuses start to develop! The joeys are born about forty days later. So every Tammar you see probably has the same birthday!

Tammars can live till they're about fourteen years old. However, as most now live in hot, dry places, such as islands, their life expectancy has been reduced. In most years about forty per cent of baby Tammars die in the long, hot summer, while many adults die at the beginning of cold, wet winters.

> **Fact**
>
> Tammars on the islands of the Houtman Abrolhos in Western Australia, where there's often no fresh water, can survive by drinking sea water.

> **Fact**
> Tammar fur is incredibly soft (the Aboriginal people used to make cloaks from them). And Tammar Wallabies were the first roos seen by European explorers (see Chapter 2).

Tammars weren't the only wallaby that Sir George Grey may have accidentally saved in his island zoo. The Parma Wallaby (*Macropus parma*) was once thought to be extinct — and then was discovered again! Once they bounded from northeastern New South Wales almost down to Victoria. But today they're classed as a 'vulnerable' species and only a few tiny populations exist.

Except in New Zealand! Sir George took the Parmas to his island in New Zealand, as well as the Tammars. By the 1960s there were so many Parmas that they had become a pest, especially to young pine plantations. Foresters tried to wipe them out until 1965 when they realised that they were killing an animal that was extinct everywhere else. Or were they?

In 1976, a female Parma Wallaby was found near Gosford in New South Wales, and since then more have been found.

Parma Wallabies are small wallabies with a greyish brown back, white throat and chest, and a very fluffy tummy. They like nice thick, moist forest, even rainforest, with some good grassy patches.

Parmas rest during the day then come out just before dusk to eat. They are great leapers, going very fast with their bodies stretched out to an almost straight line, with their tails extended behind them. They mostly live by themselves, except for joeys which live with their mums, but they can feed together in mobs.

Interestingly, on crowded Kawau Island the Parmas have become smaller than the Parmas in Australia. Even when the Kawau Parmas are taken to zoos and given better food, their babies remain small there, too.

5

A night-time roo adventure

When I first came to the valley where I live there were four kinds of wallaby: Swampies, Pretty-face Wallabies, Red-necked and Brush-tailed Rock Wallabies, as well as Eastern Grey roos. As I wandered around the bush in those days I gradually learned how each species of roo and wallaby lived, eating different foods, and the different places they occupied, even in a valley as small as this one.

I never even imagined that wild animals played games . . . not until I started to live with them, and saw joeys playing hide-and-seek with their mums, young roos splashing in the waves at Pebbly Beach or young wallabies splashing in the creek here. Young roos and joeys pretend to fight each other, too. And sometimes they pretend they are in danger from leaf shadows just to run around crazily in circles. But they don't play games like humans do.

I mostly lived by myself in those days, except at weekends. Late every afternoon I'd wash off the dirt from my day's work in the orchards, then get into clean clothes for the walk to Jean's place down the valley. Jean was a widow, and fifty-five years older than me. She baked the best sponge cake in the world for supper, made from eggs from her ducks, with cream from her cow and raspberries and passionfruit from the garden. Every evening I walked to her place, watching the animals wake up on the way down, then mooching through the bush on my way back to see what the other animals were doing. The real life of the valley only begins at night. And this was one night I'll never forget.

It was spring, but already hot, and the bush had been quiet all day. As the sun sank below the hills the birds began to call again. The sun vanishes early in our deep valley, leaving a long gentle time, not dark, but not bright sunlight either.

As I changed out of my old jeans I could see Pansy the Swampy out the bathroom window. She stood up in the middle of my herb garden, where she'd been sleeping under a wormwood bush, and scratched her tummy with her paws.

Sometimes it's hard to answer when people ask me if wallabies are friendly, or if wombats bite. It's a bit like asking if humans are cross or happy creatures. Wild animals vary a lot — just like people.

Two smaller wallabies stood up next to her. One was her joey from last year, and the other was the older joey from the year before. Pansy had another baby in her pouch too — Pansy's pouch was always bulging — but I hadn't seen it yet.

Pansy scratching her tummy

The three Swampies scratched their tummies again, then loped slowly past the house and down to the creek. I watched them bend down and sip some water, then lick their paws to help cool down after the heat of the day. Now and then they straightened up again to scratch their tummies, and then bent down to drink some more.

> **Fact**
>
> Wallabies never gulp water, no matter how thirsty they are. They know that dusk is a dangerous time, when animals like dogs or dingoes might be waiting for them to come down to drink. So they drink slowly and watchfully.

Pansy's ears swivelled to catch any new noise, and she sniffed the air, too. But the only human she could smell was me, and she was used to my smell. I might do dumb things like stay out sweating all day in the hot sunlight, planting potatoes, but I wasn't a threat to her or her babies.

Suddenly the little joey in Pansy's pouch stuck his nose out and sniffed the water. He looked a bit like a bald grey mouse. He twitched his nose then dived down into the pouch again. Mum's milk was still more interesting, he decided.

Pansy and her babies hopped back up to the garden as I sat down to pull on my boots.

Down at the creek

Each Swampy has its own territory, but the territories overlap with those of other Swampies. The creek is no-one's territory, though. All the animals, except for meat-eaters like dogs, will drink side by side at the creek. I've watched a wallaby drink standing only thirty centimetres from a red-bellied black snake that was sipping at the water too, while a mob of roos drank just a little way away as well.

Snakes are pretty good at getting out of the way if they feel vibrations in the ground from roo or wallaby feet. And roos and wallabies are pretty good at not treading on snakes. But basically they don't threaten each other, so they leave each other alone. Though I'm sure that the occasional roo or wallaby does get bitten if it blunders onto a snake that is sleeping, or disturbs one whose escape route is blocked.

Pansy and her joeys started to eat. They nibbled some grass first, mostly because it was easy to find and they were hungry after their day's sleep. Pansy's smallest baby leaned out of her pouch to nibble at grass, too — I could see him more closely now and I thought he looked more like a mouse than ever.

The joey nibbled the grass and chewed it thoughtfully. He bent to have another nibble, but it tickled his nose. He jumped back, startled, and snuggled down into Pansy's pouch again.

Pansy's bigger baby stuck his head into his mum's pouch to have a drink of milk, too. Pansy stood patiently for a few minutes, chewing a mouthful of grass, then pushed the bigger baby away. Pansy was bored with grass. It was time to look for something more interesting for breakfast. Perhaps some lemon leaves, a few rosebuds, or a bit of wonga vine . . . aha, there's the mandarin tree!

Pansy reached up and picked a mandarin with her paws. She handed one to the middle-sized joey, while the biggest joey picked one for himself. I watched the family sit there, happily guzzling mandarins, the juice running down their paws and onto their tummies. Even the baby reached up out of the pouch to have a nibble at Pansy's mandarin.

It was time for me to go. Jean would be waiting. I'd promised her some lemons, so I needed to go further up the gorge to get them, to the small orchard surrounded by rocks and cliffs and ledges.

This was Rock Wallaby territory. Swampies like the gullies near the creek, but the Rock Wallabies spend the day sheltering in small rock overhangs and caves — just one wallaby to each cave, except for mothers with their joeys.

The Rock Wallabies were coming down to drink, too. The wallabies can leap several metres from rock to rock, or jump down almost vertical cliffs and still keep their balance. But when they first wake up they're hot and sleepy, so they came down to the creek the easy way, in between the rocks. They drank slowly, like the Swampies, as I picked the bag of lemons. Then they made their way back into the rocks to nose out young shrubs and tussocks to eat.

The moon was rising now as I headed up the hill to the front gate. It was a full moon that night. The moon always looks massive when it first comes over the ridge, like it's going to bounce. I could see the line of moonlight flow up the valley as the moon climbed higher. Suddenly the whole valley was bright with silver light.

There'd be no need to use a torch tonight.

I started to walk down the road. The Red-necked Wallabies were already grazing on either side. It's a steep and winding road, just dirt and potholes and landslides when it rains, so there were only three or four cars a day travelling it unless I was having friends for lunch.

Five mobs of Red-necks lived at this end of the valley. That night there were about thirty of them all grazing together, with heads down and concentrating on their grass. Only a few of them had babies. Unlike Swampies, which almost always have a baby in their pouch, Red-necks only breed when there's lots of good grass around.

They glanced up at me, then went back to eating.

Something bounded across the hill above me. It was a pair of young Eastern Greys. The joeys woke up earlier than their parents, who had been sleeping under the trees in the paddocks up from the road, where the country is more open and grassy, a bit like a park. The grown-up roos were still standing about, yawning and scratching their tummies, but the young ones were chasing each other and pretending to wrestle. The roos hadn't bothered to get a drink yet.

I watched the big roos bend down and taste a few mouthfuls of grass, resting on their front legs, then sit up, balanced on their tails, and stare out at the valley, thoughtfully regurgitating the food they'd swallowed to chew it a second time. Now and then they licked their paws and wrists to cool themselves down.

This mob was ruled by an old 'buck' roo. Big Buck was half as tall again as the females, and was ten years old — quite old for a roo — and he might live another couple of years. There were no other big males in this mob, just some half-grown joeys.

When the male joeys are fully grown they'd either challenge Big Buck or wander off till they were bigger than he was — they hope. Usually Big Buck only had to give a ferocious 'challenge grunt' and rear up to his full height for challengers to retreat and decide that they didn't really want to rule the mob. Yet.

Big Buck stared down at me. He watched me walk down the road every night, but he still wasn't sure about me. Finally, he decided that I wasn't a threat — tonight, anyhow. But he stayed watchful. He needed to check that none of the males were anywhere near 'his' females, too. He was also checking that his mob wasn't in any danger from wild dogs and dingoes, or pet dogs off their chains, or even Wedge-tailed Eagles that might snatch a baby roo.

Suddenly, Big Buck looked up. A car was coming up the valley. I wondered who it was. The Red-necked Wallabies munching the grass beside the road stood upright too, staying perfectly still, except for their ears that swivelled as they listened. Kangaroos and wallabies have good eyesight as well as acute hearing — they need it to survive.

Big Buck thumped a warning with his feet. The other roos all looked up. Should they run? The mothers made 'tsk-tsk' sounds to warn their joeys to stay near.

The car came round the corner. I stood back in the trees' shadows near the fence to let it pass, blinking in the glare of the headlights.

The first shot just missed me. I screamed, just as the second shot jerked my arm. I waited for the pain, the blood. Another shot, and another. I screamed again, waving my arms so the shooters knew I was there. I heard one of them swear. Then they gunned the motor, and the ute sped off up the mountain road.

I was shaking, from anger as well as fright. I looked at my arm. The bullet hadn't struck me, just gone through the sleeve of my jacket. A few centimetres the other way and I'd have been dead.

I looked up at the hill. The roos were all running in different directions. Even the joeys took a different route from their mothers, to make it harder for anything to attack the whole mob.

One of the roos pushed her joey out of her pouch, under a bush where it would be hidden. She bounded down to the road where the shooters had been, to draw them away from her baby. But the hunters had gone. The Red-necks returned to the shelter of the trees. All but one.

The big roo bounded away to find her baby again. I walked up to the wounded wallaby and crouched down. It was hardly alive, its paws twitching frantically, its eyes gazing at me in terror. But as I watched the twitching stopped. The eyes seemed to cloud. She was dead. There was nothing I could do.

I hadn't recognised the ute — it wasn't a local. I waited just in case it came back again, watching the headlights travel up the mountain road. The Pretty-face Wallabies would be feeding lower down, and the Rock Wallabies further up.

I waited for more shots, or for the ute to stop, which meant that they could have hit a wallaby who'd darted out across the road in terror at the last minute. But the headlights climbed steadily up the mountain. Soon they were gone.

A few years ago I would have buried the wallaby, but now I knew that she was food for the goannas, crows and other creatures. It was best to leave her where she lay. I checked her pouch, but there wasn't a joey.

So I walked on down to Jean's.

It felt good to be safe in a lit room. But I felt angry, too. Night should be a safe time, for me and other animals, the harsh sunlight gone, the valley full of possums and wombats, owls and nightjars. The shooters had made me feel scared of the darkness. I would never walk that bit of road again without a tingle of fear. They had made me feel ashamed of being human, too.

The moon was high when I finally left Jean's, full of sponge cake and raspberries and passionfruit and cream. I was no longer shaking.

And then I saw the wallaby again. This time she wasn't alone. Another Red-neck stood next to her. He wasn't sniffing her, or grazing, either. He just stood there in the moonlight, keeping company with the dead. He watched me as I walked past — slowly, so as not to startle him. They'd been scared enough tonight.

Was he one of her joeys? A friend? One of the 'boss males' of the group? I didn't know.

There was no sign of the other Red-necks. They must have stayed in the shelter of the trees. There was little grass for them to eat there, but they may have wanted to go hungry rather than feed where their companion was shot.

I kept on walking. Even when I came to my house I didn't stop. I didn't want to go into the world of lights and doors that shut the night away. I wanted to stay with the animals, to forget I was human, like those boys in the ute, at least for a little while. I wanted to try to feel safe in the night again.

I walked up the hill, and sat on a log and looked down at the valley. I could see the roos grazing in the moonlight. A baby roo leaned out of its pouch to eat, too. Then suddenly it leaned too far and fell onto the grass. It was about to jump back in when its mum hopped away a few paces. The joey hesitated, then it began to eat again, staying close to mum.

A couple of older joeys were playing. They grasped each other around the neck, then boxed with their paws and kicked each other. Suddenly Big Buck turned and stared at them. The game had become serious. The two joeys crouched down, holding their bodies close to the ground and ducking their heads, to show that they accepted Big Buck as the boss.

I stayed sitting there in the moonlight. It was so quiet I could hear the thump, thump, thump as the mob of roos moved across the hill. Now that they had full bellies it was time to wander about a bit, to check out new feeding places, for the males to sniff the females, or just to eat more slowly, choosing the best or most interesting bits.

I sat there the whole night, on my log, just watching the valley. I heard the yells of possums arguing, the rush of air as a powerful owl glided through the trees above, the tiny flap of bats.

The moon sank low again. The dawn began to grow grey. All around me the serious eating began again, so the animals had full tummies before they slept for the day; not just the roos and wallabies, but all the creatures of the night.

The Swampies and the Rock Wallabies bounded down to the creek for another drink. Big Buck sniffed as the daylight grew. How hot would it be today? Roos can tell if it's going to be a scorcher or if a storm or rain is coming, months before. (This means that they can have joeys in their pouches ready to eat grass when a drought breaks.)

Big Buck lifted his head and gave a clucking sound. It was too soft for me to hear, but the other roos heard it. As I watched they followed Big Buck down to the creek — he must have decided that the mob would need a drink.

Fact

Roos only sweat when they're bounding along and they lose very little moisture. But on hot days they do like to drink.

Three of the females drank first, with their joeys, while Big Buck stood guard. The others stood around warily. Then another two or three drank, and then the rest.

The roos slowly bounded up the hill again, but not to the trees where they slept the night before. This was another group of trees, though it was one they used regularly. The ground was bare under the trees from their bodies.

They lay down one by one, but they kept their heads upright. Roos don't sleep soundly, like humans do. They're always aware of sounds and smells around them, ready to run away at the slightest hint of danger. Now they dozed and looked out over the valley as they regurgitated the night's grass to chew again.

The sun was above the ridges now, and the valley had shadows again. The birds were yelling above me, sticking their beaks into blossoms and hunting for insects. Somehow I felt clean again, no longer ashamed to be human, like the hunters who'd left the wallaby bleeding on the grass.

I started to walk down the hill. I could see a Rock Wallaby dozing on one of the rocks below me. As the day grew hotter it would bound back into the crevices in the rocks, where it would be hidden from dogs and foxes, and humans too. Rock Wallabies sleep more soundly than roos, though still not as soundly as humans.

As I walked through my garden gate I could see Pansy and her joeys, reaching for one last mandarin before they went to sleep. I'd planted those mandarin trees and the avocadoes that fed the wombats and wallabies, the currawongs and silver eyes through the winter. I had let the trees grow back in the cleared paddocks that now sheltered the wallabies from the sun.

And as I walked inside I knew that humans and wildlife *can* live together, if the humans decide they want to try.

Fact

Roads are warm, and moisture from rain and dew washes off onto the verges, watering the plants along the edge of the bitumen. Often when there's not much other grass around there's still good green pick next to roads. This is why so many roos, wallabies and wombats are tempted to eat there, especially late at night after most of the cars have gone. Often people think there are lots of roos (or wombats) around, because they see so many by the side of the road. But this may be the only place they're grazing for kilometres.

6

Roos growing up

Kangaroo and wallaby mothers are the most amazing in the world.

They carry their small babies with them all the time. (Okay, a few other animals do this.)

They have four teats — and each teat can give a different sort of milk to feed four babies of different ages! (No other animals can do this.)

When they are pregnant they are able to stop the development of their unborn baby until there's good food or water. (No other animal can do this, either!)

Kangaroos and wallabies have so many unique characteristics because they've had to adapt to a land of droughts, floods, bushfires and even snow storms. This has made their ways of breeding and bringing up their young very adaptable, too.

> **Fact**
> Kangaroos and wallabies have forward-opening pouches — they open at the top when they stand on their hind legs. Wombats and koalas have pouches that open backwards — they open downwards when they stand on their hind legs.

Breeding and birth

Some roos like the big Reds, Euros and Swamp Wallabies breed all year round if there's lots of good grass. But other wallabies and Grey Kangaroos only have their babies at certain times of the year, when their territory gets good rain and there's going to be lush grass to feed the mother and baby.

Kangaroos and wallabies often only have one joey each year. When it is born, it's only tw-and-a-half centimetres long, and weighs less than two grams. It does not even have eyes, ears or fur. (It looks more like a pink bean seed than something that can grow into a roo or wallaby!)

As soon as the baby comes out of the birth opening, it grabs onto its mother's fur with its tiny strong, front pink paws. It can't see or hear, but it can smell where it needs to get to — its mum's pouch. It takes about three minutes for the joey to pull itself up and into the pouch.

The tiny, hairless newborn joey quickly finds its mothers teat

Once nestled in mum's soft fur the joey puts its mouth around one of the four teats. It's too small and unformed to be able to suck yet, so mum pumps milk into the baby's mouth, while it just lies there, growing bigger and bigger.

> **Fact**
>
> Female kangaroos generally mate again a few days after the tiny baby is born. But the new 'embryo' (the very tiny, just developing, unborn baby) won't grow until the joey in the pouch decides to leave — or if it dies.

Life inside the pouch

The length of time a joey stays in its mum's pouch varies according to the species: from about 180 days for Rock Wallabies, 234 days for Red Kangaroos, 250 days for Tammar Wallabies, 265 days for Swampies, and 312 days for Grey Kangaroos.

After eight days (the times vary a bit with others) for a Grey Kangaroo joey, you can tell if it's a boy or a girl; after 67 days you can see its whiskers; and at about 154 days the joey's eyes open. At 165 days the first hair appears on the Grey roo's head, and in another ten days there's hair on its body too, though it's soft and fine, like mouse fur. In fact, the joey still looks more like a baby mouse than a kangaroo. About this time the joey is able to let go of the teat and grab hold of it again.

A newborn joey's immune system isn't properly developed. So for about a hundred days it relies on its mum's 'baby' milk to fight infection. As the joey grows the mother's milk changes so it's always exactly the sort of food the joey needs. There are more amino acids for brain development and more sulphur for first-time hair growth.

The fur keeps on growing, but the joey is still soft and pinkish. It doesn't become a definite colour until it's over six months old. Once the baby has fine fur, just long enough to be able to ruffle, it starts peering out of its mother's pouch. Soon it will decide to try whatever mum is eating.

If it's a kangaroo joey it will lean down and taste some grass; or if it's a baby wallaby its mum may use her front paws to pull down a branch with young leaves for her baby to try. Soon the joey is feeding whenever mum feeds, chomping with its head out of the pouch, then diving back down to have a drink.

As the baby gets bigger and bigger, its fur remains soft and velvety and very fine, not coarse like an adult roo or wallaby fur.

Then about three weeks after it's first started eating solid food, when it's about three or four months old, the joey will accidentally lean so far out of the pouch to grab a really good bit of grass that it will fall out, head first.

It stands up and looks around, and often it tries to jump back into the pouch. But mum will turn away, to give the baby a chance to get used to the outside world. Usually the baby decides that it's really not that scary out of the pouch, after all. It'll bend down and have a nibble of grass or leaves, staying very, very close to mum, though. If anything scares it, the joey will hop back in head first and do a sort of somersault to get its head back up.

Jumping into the pouch in a hurry can sometimes get confusing

> **Fact**
> Sometimes (not often) roos or wallabies who are racing away from dingoes, or a pack of dogs or hunters, will throw their baby out of the pouch into some dense scrub to hide it while the pursuers keep chasing the adults. If the mother is caught, then the baby may die from starvation, heat or cold, or dogs or dingoes may get it.

A world outside the pouch

As the joey gets bigger — and too heavy to carry easily — its mum will dart away if there's danger and the baby will race off in another direction.

By about seven to ten months old the joey stays out of the pouch all the time (the exact time is different for various wallabies and roos and some tolerant mums let their young stay in their pouch longer too — plus some joeys want to get out and bouncing fast).

But even when it's spending all its time out of the pouch and eating lots of grass the young wallaby or roo still sticks its head into the pouch now and then to have a drink of milk till it's almost fully grown. By now, the mother will most likely have another baby in her pouch (usually one crawls up to the pouch within a week of the older joey leaving). The big joey will use a different teat and have quite different milk from the tiny one, which needs milk suitable for a baby.

A most incredible type of milk

Tammar Wallaby milk may be the world's most effective antibiotic. It kills ninety-nine per cent of bacteria in an hour — it's a hundred times more powerful than penicillin, and kills all sorts of dangerous bacteria, like golden staph, *E. coli*, salmonella, streptococci, and even pseudomonas (antibiotic-resistant bacteria) and fungi as well.

So far this species of wallaby milk has only been tested in laboratories. For it to be sold as human medicine scientists would have to develop a formula to make artificial wallaby milk — wallabies just don't give enough milk to make human medicine, too. But one day you might just be having a small dose of wallaby milk to cure your illness — in a tablet, anyway!

Unless there's a really bad drought or bushfire most baby wallabies and roos survive their time in the pouch. But life is much more dangerous for them when they start venturing around the outside world, especially in the first few months. Humans, dogs and other predators enjoy hunting and eating roos and wallabies,

Very young joeys like to slide out of their mum's pouch and explore the world for a while.

and the young and very old animals often can't outrun them.

Female joeys tend to stay with their mums longer than male joeys, which means that a lot more male joeys die young. This is one reason why mobs of roos have more females than males.

Roos and wallabies take between one and two years before they become adults (the timing's different for different species). In years of bad drought or bushfire the females may not become mature — and able to make and have babies — until they are at least three years old.

Kangaroos and wallabies live about six to fourteen years, though some may make it up to twenty years old if they are very lucky. If they have plenty of food and water they may live much longer than they would otherwise in times of drought when grass and water are scarce.

7

Fascinating roo poo

Human babies are taught very early *not* to play with poo — or eat it either! But young joeys *need* to eat some roo poo. Roo droppings are a bit like a vitamin pill for baby roos. These tiny round droppings contain little organisms from the mother's gut that help the joey to digest tough grass. If the joey didn't eat them it might get diarrhoea and even die.

Roo poo is also fascinating if you happen to be a native dung beetle — it lives on roo, wallaby and other native animal poo. Native dung beetles love roo poo. (Horse and cattle poo is too big for Aussie dung beetles to cope with — scientists had to bring in big dung beetles to cope with giant poos.)

Adult dung beetles haul the balls of roo poo down into the soil for their young larvae to eat — and as the young dung beetles tunnel through the poo they help break it up and turn it back into soil.

The beetles with too much poo to chew

Native dung beetles evolved to eat the nice small poos of roos, wallabies and wombats. But if native dung beetles get too much dung — like lots of great big squishy cattle pats — they aren't able to break it up quickly before flies can breed in it.

By the 1960s, after so many flies had bred in big poos of animals, the CSIRO started to bring in large South African dung beetles that could manage really big poos. These beetles had adapted to dealing with really big poos like those left behind by elephants, rhinos and giraffes. And suddenly there were no longer as many flies in our eyes . . . or on sheep's bums.

Roo poo is useful

Roo and wallaby poo is incredibly useful even if you're not a dung beetle. When roos and wallabies eat grass they also eat the seeds. And when the weather's dry — which it often is — and the grass dies, those seeds are kept safe in the roo poo until it rains again. Then the poo dissolves, the seeds germinate and more grass grows again. Without roo and wallaby poo even more of Australia would be a desert.

Roo and wallaby poo also contains micro-organisms and fungi that return to the soil to help

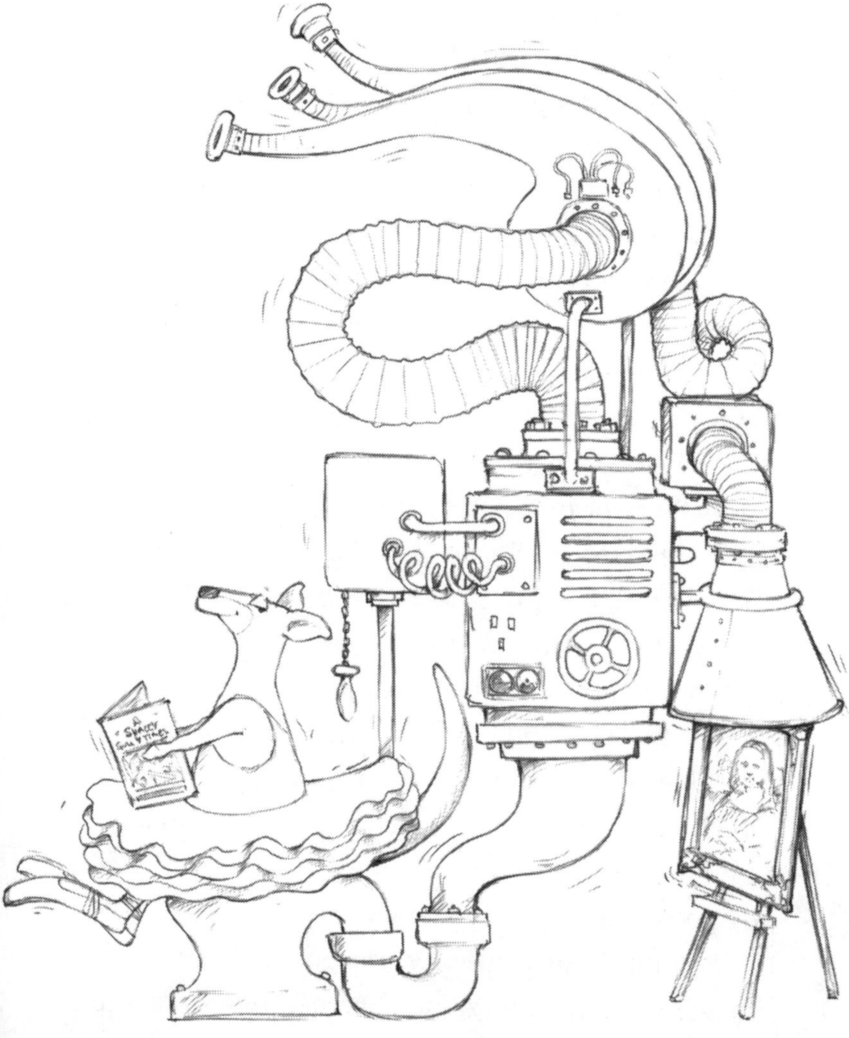

control pests and, of course, feeds the soil so plants can grow — roo poo is an all-round fertiliser.

Roo poo is also great if you want to know exactly who was out on 'your' grass last night, and how many of them there were. Just pick up the dung — or bend down and look at it closely — and you'll be able to tell what type of animal left it. And if there is lots of dung, you know there were lots of animals!

Roo poo can be used in other ways, too. Some Aboriginal nations used dry roo or wallaby poo to light their fires. They'd cut open a dry branch and put dry roo poo inside. Then they'd rapidly twist a spear thrower or other stick in the poo until it heated up and burst into flames. In other places roo poo was used a bit like firelighters, to bring fire from one campfire to another that was a long way away.

Dry roo poo was threaded onto a stick and held in a fire till the end caught alight. The poo would smoulder for about an hour, burning very, very slowly. But when anyone blew on it the extra oxygen would make it burst into flame ... and the burning roo poo could be used to light a fire somewhere else.

In central Australia dry roo poo was mixed with grass-tree resin and ground charcoal to make a strong glue to fasten sharp rock blades onto handles for axes, spears and other tools.

Even today there are some great things you can do with roo poo. But don't collect more than a few pellets of roo (or wallaby) poo from the bush. It's very valuable for the environment! But if you have a wildlife park nearby they may have too much roo or wallaby poo, and might give you some.

How to handle roo poo

Will you get sick if you touch roo poo? Any organic material — something which has once lived, like lawn clippings or yesterday's lunch — will have bacteria and fungi that may make you sick. But it's pretty unlikely, as healthy humans are good at coping with everyday-type bacteria and fungi.

Roo poo is a pretty safe material to work with, too. It doesn't stink like a meat-eater's poo, and it's dryish. In fact, it's mostly just digested grass and leaves. But, yes, you should apply some basic hygiene practice around roo poo!

- Always wear gloves when handling roo poo.
- Don't touch your face with your roo poo gloves. (Take them off if you need to blow your nose!)
- Don't touch food or drink with roo poo gloves, or anywhere food or drink is prepared. (Take off the gloves and wash your hands before having food or drink.)
- Keep roo poo in a sealed container or plastic bag when you're not using it. And make sure

no-one thinks your roo poo collection is yummy choc coated sultanas and tries to eat them!

What roo poo is that?

If you consider yourself a bit of a scientist and like the idea of being able to distinguish roo and wallaby poo from other animal dung, then follow these steps to help you get started.

Look at how big the dung is

The first thing to do when you find some dung is to look at its size. Bigger animals leave bigger lumps, pellets, piles and cakes of dung, so a roo's dung is bigger than a wallaby's, and a wallaby's dung is bigger than a rabbit's.

But when the grass is soft and green, lush poos — or scats or droppings — will be bigger than when all the feed is dry. And when the grass is green the dung of grass-eaters is often stuck together, instead of in separate pellets, so the scats look bigger. But if you look closely you'll see that they are still made up of small bits stuck together.

Work out the shape and colour of the dung

Roo and wallaby dung are oval black pellets, round at each end but not as perfectly round as sheep poo. Sometimes there are only a few pellets, other times as

Quokkas leave small rounded pellets

Wallaby droppings are smaller than roo droppings, and contain bits of fruit, leaves or twigs as well as grass

Possum droppings are small and usually under trees or by water

Roo dung are round pellets in dry times. When there's lush grass they're joined together. If you break them up they'll look like compressed chewed up grass

Cat droppings smell of cat — or canned cat food. Feral cat droppings may contain fur or feathers

Wombat droppings are much more square than roo or wallaby droppings, and chunkier, though in lush wet times they can be green and longer or sloppier

Dog droppings are usually long. If you break them up with a stick they may be like concentrated cereal, if the dog eats dry dog food, or smell of meat or canned dog food. Wild dogs may have bits of fur in their droppings

many as twelve and often in a little clump. And sometimes, when the grass is young, pellets are softer and rather squashily joined together — but whether it's hard or soft, roo and wallaby poo will only smell of sweet grass and have a grassy texture.

Most roo and wallaby droppings look pretty much alike, though there are enough differences for an expert to be able to tell one from another. Generally, if it's an open grassy area it's more likely roo or Euro dung than wallaby. And if there's lots of dung scattered about it's probably roo dung, as they mob together, or a species of wallaby that grazes in mobs.

There are also only a few animals which have round poos. Goat and sheep dung are round and black like roo and wallaby dung, and in wet green years the round pellets may be stuck together. Rabbit dung is round, though it's smaller than roo or wallaby dung, and usually left in small piles (roos and wallabies don't leave their dung in piles).

Look inside the dung

Break open the dung with a stick to see what the animal has been eating. This is the best way to tell exactly what animal it comes from — even if it's a bit messy!

If it's black on the outside and a yellowy colour inside it's probably roo or wallaby dung. That's because roos and wallabies are *very* good about getting all of the moisture out of their food, so their poo is usually drier, not as moist and dark inside. Kangaroo or wallaby poo usually will have finely chopped bits of grass in it.

Wallaby poos have tiny points at one end, too, and sometimes have fibres sticking out because they eat coarser material like leaves and shoots. Roos mostly eat grass, so they won't have any fibres in their poos.

Make a poo collection

During the last century rich hunters used to collect the heads of the animals they'd shot and then they'd have them stuffed by a taxidermist and hang them on their walls as trophies. If you like the idea of learning to track wild animals — but don't want to hurt or kill them — why not make a dung collection?

Collect as many different sorts of dung as you can. Cover them in clear nail polish to help preserve them, then glue or pin them onto white cardboard, with notes about which animal the dung is from, where it lives, where you collected it and at what time of year.

If you think you may have found the dung of a rare wallaby that no-one knows about, ring your local museum or national parks office. They'll be able to tell you who to send it to and how, so that someone can tell what animal it came from. Don't cover any possibly rare dung in nail varnish. Instead wrap it in clean greaseproof paper and keep it in a jar.

What Poo Can Tell You

Scientists — zoologists who study animals — can tell a lot from poo!

- the number of droppings will tell you how many animals are around — as long as you know how many droppings each species puts out each night.
- droppings can tell a scientist what the animal has been eating
- parasite eggs, bacteria and viruses as well as blood, hormones, minerals and other things in droppings help a scientist to know whether the animals might have something wrong with them

Fact

Roo and wallaby poo can tell geologists if there may be precious metals around. Deep tree roots bring up minerals from under the earth, and grass roots bring up minerals nearer the surface. The roos and wallabies eat the grass or leaves, and poo out the minerals in their droppings.

So if you find gold or silver in your roo poo, there may be treasure under the ground.

8

How to move like a kangaroo

Do you know what's the most efficient way in the world to move? In a car? No way. Swim like a whale? Gallop like a horse? None of these.

Scientists have concluded that the most efficient way to travel is like a big Red Kangaroo (and pretty much the same way all other roos and wallabies move, too).

Australia can get *very* dry and, to survive, roos and wallabies often have to travel vast distances with little food or water, using the smallest amount of energy possible.

Boundless energy

Kangaroos use less energy to travel than any other animals. They use less water, too, because their amazing internal system can cool them down.

How do they do it? Well, hopping allows the kangaroo to recapture the energy of each bound, in the tendons of its legs. Boing! boing! ... and every boing propels their legs forward into the next bound. Their heavy, muscular tail keeps roos and wallabies steady too, so that they can just keep going, fast, without having to slow down to balance and lose all that lovely forward motion.

That's not all. Every leap a roo takes pushes its gut back, drawing air into its lungs — and this saves even more energy. Which makes the kangaroo the best-designed traveller in the world.

But kangaroos and wallabies can move in several ways. The way most of us know is when they leap on their powerful hind legs, with their great long feet, using their tails for balance. A kangaroo leaping this way can hop up to 64 kph and leap up to two metres high.

But roos and wallabies don't only leap in great long bounds. The way they move depends on what they're doing. If they are feeding and only need to move slowly they can walk on all fours, too. They balance on their front paws and tail, and sort of swing their back legs forward. And if they are about

A bounding kangaroo can't move its legs independently as humans do. The roo's strong back legs propel it forwards.

to fight they may shuffle forward using just their back legs and tail, but without a proper leap.

If they need to go fast they leap in great long bounds. Interestingly if a roo is bounding between 15 and 35 kph it performs about the same number of hops per minute, as it does when it's going faster — it's just that as it gets faster each hop is longer. However when roos need to go really fast, say over 40 kph, they take even longer hops and do more hops per minute.

Roos can't walk or hop backwards much, because their legs are the wrong shape and their tail gets in the way. When moving about on land they can only move their back legs together at the same time, too, not one at a time like we do — except for Tree-kangaroos, which can move their hind legs one by one when they climb. However, when kangaroos are swimming they can kick each leg independently (*see* also page 148).

Fact

Kangaroos usually don't travel much — they generally live and die within a few kilometres of the territory where they're born. They *can* survive long journeys, but mostly don't bother, especially if there's enough food in their area. If there isn't, they just stop having babies until the grass grows again, rather than move away.

Horsepower or roo-power?

A large kangaroo can leap nine metres in a single bound! That's longer than many rooms! But which is faster, a kangaroo or a horse?

A roo can accelerate from standing still to whoosh! faster than a horse. And over a short distance a big kangaroo can bound faster than a horse. (I've timed roos bounding along next to my car at our place at about 50 kph.) But kangaroos can't keep that speed up for as long as a horse can.

On the other hand, roos use less energy as they run than a horse, and are able to keep cool better. But a horse can carry a much heavier load than a roo.

If I had to travel a hundred kilometres I'd rather be a roo than a horse. But I think I'd put my money on a horse, rather than a roo, to win the Melbourne Cup.

Deciphering roo and wallaby tracks

You can tell by a roo's or wallaby's tracks how fast it has been going.

When roos have been bounding along you'll see big hind tracks side by side. If the prints are far apart the roo has been going fast — maybe escaping from shooters. But if the prints are close together the roo has gone more slowly. You sometimes see where the tail has thumped down briefly behind, too.

Wallabies leave different tracks. A slow-moving wallaby leaves two tracks side by side and a long tail print behind. The tail print can look a bit like a snake track. But snakes usually don't leave tracks as deep as that. If you see small hind prints and no tail imprint it's probably a wallaby in a hurry.

If roos or wallabies have been grazing in an area you'll see long back footprints and small front paw prints when they were balancing on their front paws and tail, and lifting their back legs to swing them forward.

Fact

Animals' paths through the bush will tell you how big the animal was that made them. Humans make tall tracks as we push through bushes. Wombats make low tracks so any bush higher than a wombat's back will be undisturbed. Wallabies are taller so the path they make is higher too.

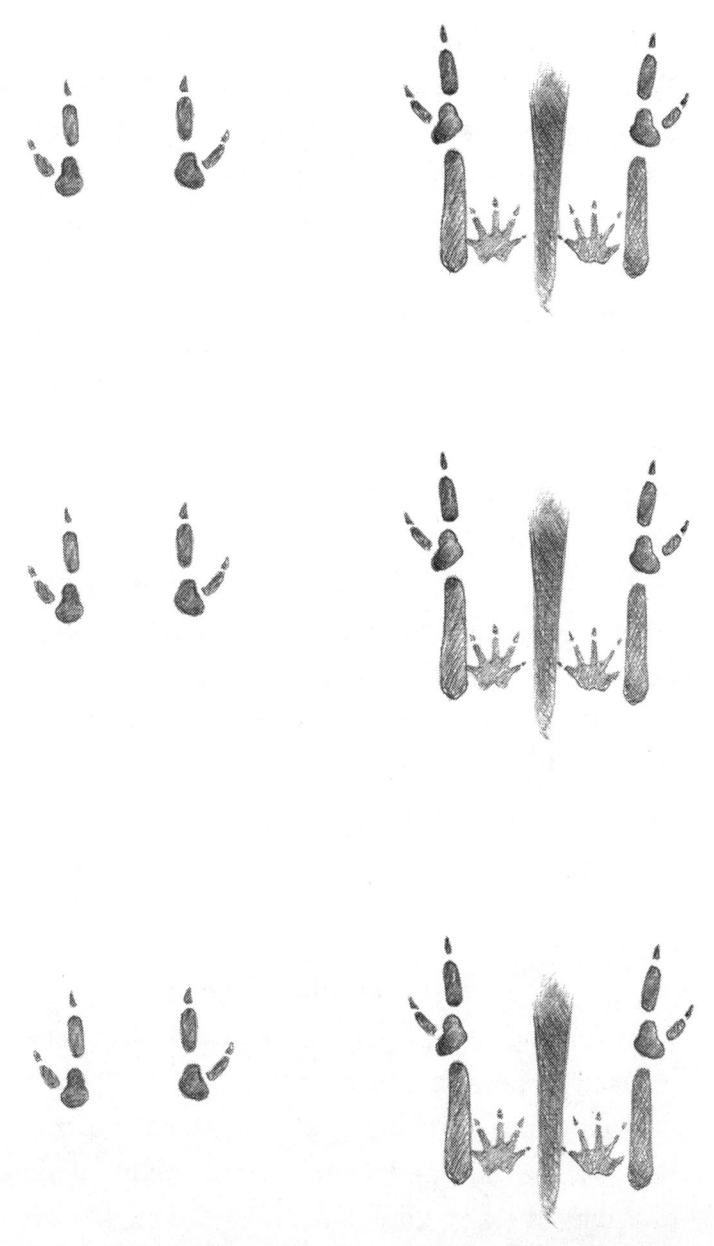

Prints left by a wallaby in a hurry

Prints left by a slow-moving, grazing roo

The amazing surfing roos

Roos and wallabies can swim, though they mostly don't. Sometimes they *have* to swim to get away from dogs or dingoes. Even though roos and wallabies can only move their back legs together when they're on land, when they swim they can kick with each leg.

Sometimes roos and wallabies just want to swim. After a long drought when the creek had been dry for years I once watched a wallaby jump in and swim across the creek for the sheer pleasure of being in lots of water. It got out, shook itself, then jumped in and swam back again!

The roos at Pebbly Beach on the south coast of New South Wales go into the surf at the end of a long hot day to cool off — a wonderful sight to see. But I've never seen the ones at Merry Beach (about twenty kilometres away) do more than paddle along the edge. (I'd love to know if anyone has seen other groups of roos surfing.)

Staying cool like a kangaroo

Roos manage to stay cool in Australia's very hot climate. So how do they do it?

Roos and wallabies mostly sleep during the heat of the day and come out at night, which is one way to keep cool. But even the nights can be hot in summer.

Humans sweat to cool down, because as the sweat evaporates it cools the skin. Roos and wallabies sweat, too, but mostly only when they are bounding along. Sweating uses up a lot of water, and there often isn't much water around for roos and wallabies to drink.

One brilliant way that roos and wallabies keep cool is by licking their paws and wrists. Roo and wallaby skin is thinner on their forearms than on the rest of their body, and the blood vessels are very close to the surface. As the saliva evaporates it cools the outside skin — so the heat goes from their body onto the skin then gets cooled down. Licking also uses much less water than sweating does.

> **Fact**
>
> If your car scares a roo or wallaby and it bounds off, ask the driver to stop and then watch what happens. As soon as the roo is no longer terrified it will stop and lick its paws to cool itself down. Roos and wallabies also pant to cool down.

Both roos and wallabies look for the coolest spots to camp, too. Big Reds camp under the shade of trees, usually near the top of hills where there's some breeze. (If you want to find the coolest place around to have a picnic, look for where the roos are sheltering. Then picnic somewhere else — the roos won't want to be disturbed!)

Rock Wallabies and Wallaroos look for crevices in rocks or caves or the shade of piles of boulders. Nailtail Wallabies make depressions under bushes. Quokkas look for bushes to shelter under, too.

Swampies are great at finding the coolest spot, often by a fence or down in a gully. Lying on damp, shady ground is especially cooler.

In winter, roos and wallabies look for sun-warmed spots, such as hot rock ledges, or on bare ground under trees that feels warm on their skin, even though they're sheltered from the sunlight, too. You'll often find roos or wallabies basking in the sun after a frosty night.

Roos and wallabies don't like rain, either, or hail or snow — they are very good at finding shelter from them. One way to tell if there's going to be a thunderstorm is to watch the roos or wallabies. If they all suddenly vanish you know it's going to be a whopper.

But where have they gone? Sometimes it's under a tree with a dense canopy. If the wind is blowing strongly, it's behind a wooden fence, or a wire fence where long grass or bracken has made a screen to shelter them from the wind and rain. Sometimes they decide to visit humans, too . . .

The story of roos who came in from the cold

It was a dark and stormy night — just like in a horror story. The wind yelled down from the hills. The cold rain drummed on the roof. Suddenly there was a thump at the door.

Sharon opened the door . . .

Five roos stood on the veranda. They were large, wet, and smelled very strongly of damp kangaroo. The first one gave her a little grunt, then pushed past her. It bounded slowly down the corridor, then into the living room. The others followed it.

Sharon blinked. There's not much you can do when you're alone in a house and five perfectly strange roos decide to come in out of the dark. She tiptoed down the corridor after them.

The first roo was lying on the carpet in front of the fire. It looked very much at home. And suddenly she recognised it. Five years ago she'd raised a tiny orphaned joey. Then one day it simply took off into the bush.

'Er . . . Joseph?' she asked.

The roo looked at her vaguely as though to say, 'Yes, we did know each other once, didn't we?' Then it turned back to the fire.

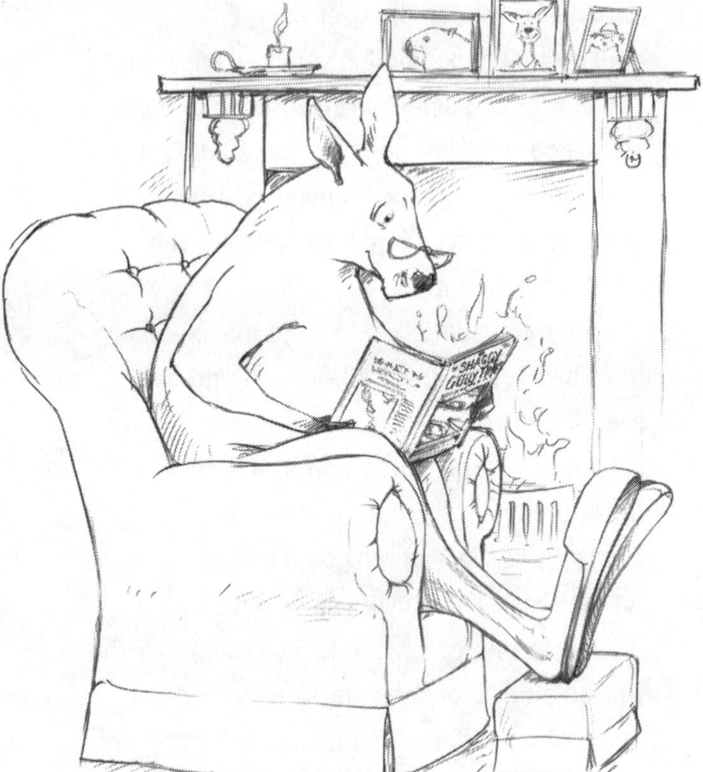
SHAGGY
GULLY

Meanwhile the other roos made themselves comfortable too, lying on the carpet. The now wet, muddy carpet.

Sharon wasn't sure what to do. Should she offer them a snack? But what did you offer five enormous kangaroos? Besides, they looked quite content.

So she sat down and began to read again. Every now and then she glanced at the roos to make sure they were really there. They were. And, besides, the room was starting to smell very strongly of kangaroo.

An hour passed and then another. Sharon was wondering if she could go to bed. The storm outside was dying down. The rain had stopped, and even the wind was settling.

Suddenly one of the roos stood up. It leaned back on its tail and scratched its chest. Its fur was dry now and slightly fluffy. Then it turned and began to hop down the corridor.

Sharon ran after it and opened the door. The roo bounded out without even looking at her. One by one the others followed.

Sharon shut the door. She said she would never have believed it had happened, if it hadn't been for the mud on the carpet. And the lingering smell of kangaroo.

And every cold wet evening since she has been waiting for the thump at the door and a mob of roos who've heard of this nice warm place, where a kangaroo can shelter on a stormy night.

9

Roos and you

Most wild animals don't like being around humans. Humans often have dogs with them, and even the smell of dogs scares many wild animals. After all, dogs eat meat and like to hunt, and most don't care if their food comes from a can or hops along in the bush for them to hunt and catch.

Humans also try to attract a roo when they spot one by treating it like a pet. They yell, 'Hey, look! Here, roo, roo, roo!' and run after it, which would frighten any animal that's not used to being around humans. (Or even me, come to think of it.)

Where kangaroos hang out

Most people only see wildlife in zoos (when the animals often asleep, or bored). But roos — and some wallabies — are much easier to see than wombats or echidnas.

Kangaroos love grass — the shorter, greener and sweeter it is the better. And humans are good at growing grass. We call it 'lawn' or 'parks' or 'golf courses'. So you can often see roos grazing in gardens near the bush.

Roos aren't quite as scared of humans as most other wildlife because kangaroos (and some wallabies) can bound very fast and can be pretty sure of getting away from dogs or yelling humans fairly quickly. Kangaroos also have a lookout scout to keep watch and thump on the ground — or just start fleeing — if there is any sign of danger about.

Kangaroos also roam further than animals like wombats to find new grass. So if there's a nice green lawn about they may just find it.

All this means that if you live on a farm, or on the outskirts of a village, and if you've got lovely short grass — and not too many cars or savage dogs about — you may have semi-tame mobs of kangaroos grazing in your garden.

Roos especially like places where there are lots of holiday homes — masses of green lawns but not too many people at any one time, except in the holidays. And, even then, many holiday-makers don't bring their dogs with them. In fact, roos can get *too* used to humans.

The story of the salad sandwiches

It was many years ago, on one of those sudden warm spring days when you begin to dream of surfing again, or at least paddling, a friend and I decided we'd head down to the coast for a picnic and a bushwalk along the headlands up from Pebbly Beach.

I picked oranges and mandarins and Val made the sandwiches, mostly with salad from her garden — grated carrot and beetroot and lettuce, and some of our avocadoes with lots and lots of homemade mayonnaise.

The beach was beautiful (and still is) — a great sweep of short green grass rolling down to the beach, with mobs of roos lying in the shade of scattered trees. We decided we'd eat lunch first then head off around the headlands.

We sat down in an unoccupied bit of shade near the rocks. Val unpacked the sandwiches . . . and suddenly there was a furry face peering between us, sniffing at the sandwiches.

It was an Eastern Grey Kangaroo — a big one — perhaps two metres high with weightlifter's muscles and a smell that was very strong and distinct of a Big Male Roo.

Val was just lifting a sandwich to her mouth when suddenly she wasn't any more — the sandwich was heading up to the roo's mouth

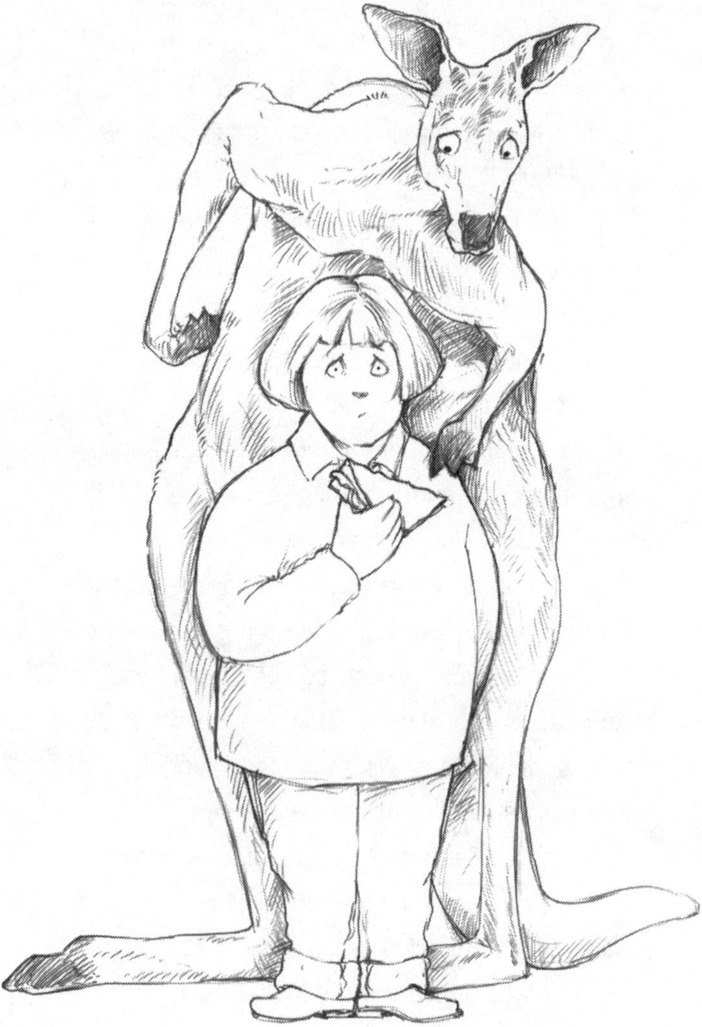

instead, in the roo's paws. He took a bite, chewed thoughtfully, then took another.

'I think he likes salad sandwiches,' said Val.

When a two-metre tall kangaroo decides he wants your meal you have two choices: share it, or move.

We decided to move. We both knew how bad bread is for roos. Besides, there was a look in this roo's eye that said his idea of sharing was four sandwiches for him and none for us.

We shifted round to another tree. Opened the basket again. I took out a sandwich . . . just as the furry paws reached down, and grabbed it from my hand. This time the roo used both paws to stuff it in his mouth, then reached down and scratched his tummy.

Two sandwiches left.

'Right,' said Val. 'You take one, I'll take the other, and we run and eat at the same time.'

So we did. I could hear the lazy bounds behind us. I'd eaten almost all of the sandwich when there was a sharp cough behind me.

In case you don't speak roo, this means, 'Give me that sandwich or I'll disembowel you with one swift slash of my claw.'

I stopped. I held out my hands with the last crust of sandwich.

The roo bent down and ate the last of the crust

from my hand. He sniffed over my fingers, just in case there were some crumbs he had missed.

A salad sandwich with avocado and homemade mayonnaise was the best thing he'd ever eaten.

He sniffed up my arm, just in case I'd hidden a sandwich in my armpit. Then he sniffed at my pockets, which made me think that a lot of picnickers had fed this roo, or brought him bread in their pockets.

And then, very slowly, so as not to startle me, he bent down and slowly licked all around my mouth, just to get the last taste of that delicious mayonnaise. There wasn't much I could do, except stand very, very still and let him do exactly what he wanted to.

Meanwhile, Val had come up with the picnic basket. The roo left me and sniffed inside the basket again. Nothing, except for six mandarins and six oranges. But the roo didn't like oranges, so looked at us threateningly.

'Time to walk,' said Val.

We started to walk. The roo followed us.

We ran. He bounded after us in long, easy strides, sure that somehow we were smuggling more of those wonderful salad and mayonnaise sandwiches somewhere.

There was only one thing for it. We dumped the basket and took to the water.

It was cold. We splashed and tried to forget our chattering teeth. The roo loped up and down in the shallow water for a while, then bounded back to a tree just above the sand, where he could lie back and watch us.

We stayed in the water till our toes were numb and the roo looked like he was dozing. Then we crept out, grabbed the basket and raced back to the car. Our boots squelched as we ran.

We were too wet to bushwalk, and too scared in case we started out and found a two-metre tall roo had decided to join us.

So we left, cursing every tourist who decided to feed a kangaroo bits of bread, and had taught this one that humans mean food.

It turned out that we were lucky. A few months later someone was badly clawed by a kangaroo near where we'd been. The national parks service quickly moved the worst offenders (the roos sadly, not the tourists who'd been feeding them) to a new site, and put up big 'Do Not Feed' signs all around the picnic area. And though some tourists still do feed the roos the problem is nowhere near as bad as it once was.

But I have always wondered if somewhere there is a giant roo, still dreaming of the magic taste of homemade mayonnaise and avocado . . .

Good manners around roos and wallabies

Roos love big grassy parks, reserves, picnic or camp grounds — especially near the bush, the beach or rivers. Kangaroos are even tempted to graze on short grass near humans having a picnic or barbecue. Gradually, the roos can get very used to humans.

It's a privilege to be able to watch roos going about their everyday lives, munching grass or sleeping in the shade of trees, or to see a mother feeding her baby or a joey peering out of its pouch. But it can be dangerous too, for both roos and people.

Roos can attack humans, especially if you get too close, or if a big male feels threatened. It's important to remember that kangaroos are *always* wild animals, even when they seem tame.

In the nineteenth century many more humans lived close to wildlife and knew how wild animals like roos behave. Nowadays very few of us live with wild animals long enough to really know them. So how should we behave around kangaroos and wallabies? Here are some useful tips.

Don't get too close!

You wouldn't like someone barging into your living room and staring at you while you ate dinner, or coming into your bedroom when you were trying to sleep. Roos and wallabies deserve privacy when eating and sleeping, too.

Look at roos and wallabies from a distance, but if they start staring at you and looking worried, back off.

Don't *ever* go close to a big male roo who is sniffing a female roo or mating. Stay away from any male that's looking threatening, too! The big roo may decide that you're a threat and will attack you — just like it would attack any male roo that comes too close. Another roo would know to give a small polite cough and back off. And they'd know that if they didn't give this polite cough the other roo would attack.

Don't expect a polite human cough to work, either. It might help. But chances are you won't do it properly, and might just make the big roo even angrier.

A male roo looks threatening when:

- it's standing tall, leaning back on its tail and looking like it's going to start boxing. It may be about to attack you;
- it's making boxing movements (or fighting another roo — look out, too);
- it's hopping slowly on all fours, with its back arched right up. It's trying to look frightening (other roos would be frightened and stay away, so you should too);
- it rubs its chest over the grass, tussocks or branches. This means it's also rubbing its scent on them — it also means, 'Hey, this is my place. Go away or I'll attack.'

Stay away from a mother with a joey in her pouch
Usually female roos and wallabies aren't aggressive, even when they have babies. But they can be. Most mums can get fierce if you threaten their babies!

Take care around roos reared by humans
Domesticated roos may have learned to box or wrestle with their carers when they were small. Now that they are big they may still want to wrestle and may hurt you — or even kill you — without realising that you are a poor weak human who doesn't know how to kangaroo fight.

Don't look at a threatening kangaroo
If a kangaroo comes up to you, look down and move away slowly. Don't yell at it to scare it away — it may think that you are going to attack it and it will attack you first! Even if you are pretty sure that the roo is just after food, move away — slowly — *without looking at it or meeting its eye*. A direct look is a challenge!

Don't feed roos or wallabies
There are many reasons for this. If you feed them the wrong food they may get sick or die or go blind. One of the most common illnesses of roos that are fed by humans is called lumpy-jaw. The roos get a swelling and abscesses on their gums. Their teeth fall out and they then starve to death.

Even feeding roos things that they can eat, like carrots or sweet potato, can be bad, because it teaches the roos that humans will give them food.

If a big male roo gets angry because humans *aren't* giving him any food he might attack. A big male roo can lift you up with one foot, and rip you open with the other. (I once watched a roo lift up a man by his jumper. The roo then ripped the man's jumper and shirt right down to his waist. If he hadn't been wearing a jumper his chest would have been ripped open instead — and he'd have been dead, or at least a challenging surgical problem.)

If park rangers think that roos and wallabies must be fed, say after a bushfire, they put out food when the animals aren't around, so they don't associate humans with tucker.

Wild animals often get to depend on human food in school holidays when there are lots of tourists about. Then suddenly there are no tourists . . . and no food. The animals starve.

In other words, look at roos and wallabies from a distance. But don't pat, and don't feed!

What to do if a roo attacks

1. Try to move away slowly, with your head down, crouching slightly to look like a roo that is accepting the big roo as boss. Give a soft cough at the same time. Don't run! The roo can run faster than you can — and he can catch you up, grab you and (worst-case scenario) disembowel you.
2. If the roo keeps coming, climb a tree or get behind a fence or indoors quickly.
3. If there's no tree, fence or building nearby, lie down quickly and roll into a ball, with your arms over your front and your hands over your face. Then yell for help. Don't panic! The roo will give up when he sees you on the ground. Wait at least ten minutes, then crawl away. Don't stand up and *don't* look directly at the roo. Just peer at him with your head down to make sure he isn't going to attack again. He will be keeping an eye on you, though, so you will have to be extremely careful.

I may have made you think that roos are dangerous animals, but they're not. They're only dangerous occasionally — and only if you don't know what to do. If humans are sensible we can share the world with roos and no-one, human or roo, will be hurt. And being with wild animals is one of the greatest joys I know.

10

How to watch roos and wallabies safely

Indigenous hunters knew how to hunt roos without being seen. These days you too can learn to track roos and wallabies to share their world. You just need to learn some of the skills below, like moving quietly, standing very still, and not looking directly at the roos.

Seeing roos and wallabies in the wild is nothing like seeing them on television or at the zoo!

If you really want to know how roos and wallabies live, you need to be with them, in their territory, where they feel at home. Roos and wallabies in wildlife parks and zoos behave very differently from wild animals. I would too if I was kept locked up, even if it was in a big paddock not a cage!

How to find roos and wallabies in your area

So what are the chances of seeing roos and wallabies in your own neighbourhood? You might not find one in your own backyard, but by following the steps below you might not have to travel as far as you think.

Ring up your local National Parks office

National park rangers and staff can tell you where to look for roos and wallabies, but especially the kind of places in that district that roos or wallabies live in. You'll also need to tell the rangers how much effort you want to make to see the animals.

Do you just want to see roos while you have a picnic? Or do you want to go on a half-hour bushwalk where you might see roos or wallabies? Or even an overnight bushwalk where the wildlife will be all around you as you camp?

In many parts of Australia there are big nature reserves where wildlife live surrounded by fences to keep out cats, dogs and foxes. These areas are a bit like zoos in one way — you know the animals will be there because they can't get over the fence. But the animals probably have no idea that they're fenced in. For them, it's still just the sort of life they enjoy. And people, like you and me, can walk through these areas without disturbing the wildlife, and be pretty sure that we'll see some animals, even on a half-hour walk.

Work out where you might see them
Use the 'Who's who' section at the back of this book to find out what species of roo or wallaby you are likely to see in your surrounding area. If you're looking for Rock Wallabies, for example, look for areas where there are sheltered rock ledges, rocky overhangs or caves. Then seek out furry dust or piles of droppings. During the day wallabies are probably asleep, and you may surprise them. (On the other hand, it's a lot more polite — and kinder — to let them sleep.)

Many wallabies seem a lot less timid than kangaroos — they don't bound away from you at once. Instead they hope they are so well camouflaged that you won't see them if they stand still. Wallabies will often stay motionless until you have gone past them, then as soon as they can see your back they'll dart in the opposite direction. Roos, on the other hand, are more likely to bound away at once.

Work out when you might see them
Big Reds, for example, are easily seen when they're resting in the shade during the day. You can also look for bare spots where roos may have been sleeping. But it can be very hard to spot wallabies sleeping under bushes or under rock overhangs or in caves.

All animals are likely to be near water, especially at dawn and dusk when they come to have a drink.

And dawn and dusk is the favourite eating time for many wild animals, too, so you may see wallabies feeding in open grassy areas, then.

Get used to darkness
Most roos and wallabies are nocturnal. If you want to see them doing something — not just resting — then you need to go out at night, or at least dusk or dawn.

One way to see roos and wallabies at night is to go 'spotlighting' — walking with a torch — when the animals are feeding. Even better, walk on nights when there is a bright full moon, and no clouds in the sky. You may find it light enough to walk without a torch, so you are less likely to scare the animals with your light. (Though you should take a torch with you anyway, as there'll be dark spots where you'll need it, and it's reassuring, too.)

During mid-summer, when it's very hot, many animals stay asleep until it cools down. This can be several hours after it gets dark. So don't be disappointed if you don't see any animals at dusk if it's been a hot day. In mid-summer, the best time to see roos and wallabies is the early mornings, when it's light but the sun still isn't up. And in mid-winter, when it's cold, the late afternoons and early evenings are often the best times, because it's still warm and comfortable for the animals to feed.

> **Fact**
> Animals seem less wary at night, perhaps because they are feeding, or they know the night is their world, just as the day is ours.

Learn when you **won't** *see them*

Like humans, roos and wallabies don't like rain much. They'll stay under shelter when it is raining rather than feed, unless they are very hungry. But if rain continues for more than three days they'll be hungry enough to go and feed despite the wet.

Roos and wallabies hate hail and thunderstorms, too — and they really hate snow. So don't bother getting cold or wet or risk being hit by lightning. Wait until the weather clears and the animals come out again. The first night after a few rainy days is a great time to see wild animals.

How to find your way around at night

The more you walk at night the more your eyes will adapt to the dark. Try it. When you first go outside at night you'll think you can't see anything at all. Then after a few minutes you'll start to make out shapes, and even colours. The longer you are in the dark, the more you'll be able to see. Here are some tips to help you in the dark.

Avoid using a torch
Try not to walk with your torch on; just keep it aside for emergencies. If you do need to turn it on, don't look straight at the bright light, or it may take half an hour for your eyes to recover their 'night sight'. (But don't fall into any holes, either. Make sure the land is safe before you try walking in the dark!)

Focus on the ground
Look at the ground when you walk at night, not the sky. The sky is lighter than you think — even if there isn't a moon — and your eyes won't adapt as well. Look straight at the ground to guide you along the path (and to also help you not to trip).

Feel the earth beneath your feet
Learn to feel the ground with your feet, so you gradually won't need to see the ground. Put your heel down first, slowly and firmly, and then let the rest of your foot follow. (You may think you do this already — walk a few steps and you'll see you don't.)

Find other ways to 'see' at night
Our eyes are only one of the senses that we can use to tell us where we're going. Use your ears, too. Can you hear water flowing? Or the rustle of leaves that will tell you where trees and bushes are? The wind sounds different on ridges and down in gullies, too.

Use your skin. If you change direction you'll realise the feel of the wind on your face has changed.

Use your nose. Things often smell more strongly at night. When I walk at night in my valley there are thousands of different smells that tell me where I am — a strong wombat smell near a burrow, the scent of gum trees, or casaurina trees, or hot grass on the hills.

Don't expect this to happen in one night, though. It takes years to learn to do it well, so have patience.

How to avoid scaring roos and wallabies away

Kangaroos that hang around picnic areas are used to humans, so they won't take much notice of you. They'll just keep on eating, sleeping, scratching or feeding their babies — as long as you don't do something dumb, like run up to them and start yelling.

But roos and wallabies in other places will think of you as another strange animal and are going to be scared when you suddenly appear. So you need to know how to reassure them that you don't mean them any harm.

Be very quiet

The bush is a quiet place. Any loud noise you hear, like a kookaburra's laugh, is really an alarm call telling other birds and animals that there are strangers or there's danger around. Or else it's a challenge call to other birds. Any bird or animal who hears a loud noise in the bush is going to be wary. So shhhhhhhh!

Move very slowly
Wild animals only move fast if there's danger or if they're hunting other animals. So if you run towards a roo or wallaby, they will think, 'Aha! They want to eat me!' And they'll run away. Wallabies and roos have learned that if you're not wary, you're dinner.

Don't look directly at them
Hunting animals look straight at the dinner they're trying to catch. Other animals in the bush don't stare at each other. Instead, put your head down so that your chin is nearly on your chest. Look up, just with your eyes. You'll still be able to see the animals, but you won't seem to be staring.

Go in disguise yourself
You need to disguise that you are a human. No, don't try dressing up as a roo, because real roos will know you're not!

Humans are hunters, and they have eyes like meat-eating hunters. The eyes of roos and wallabies are on

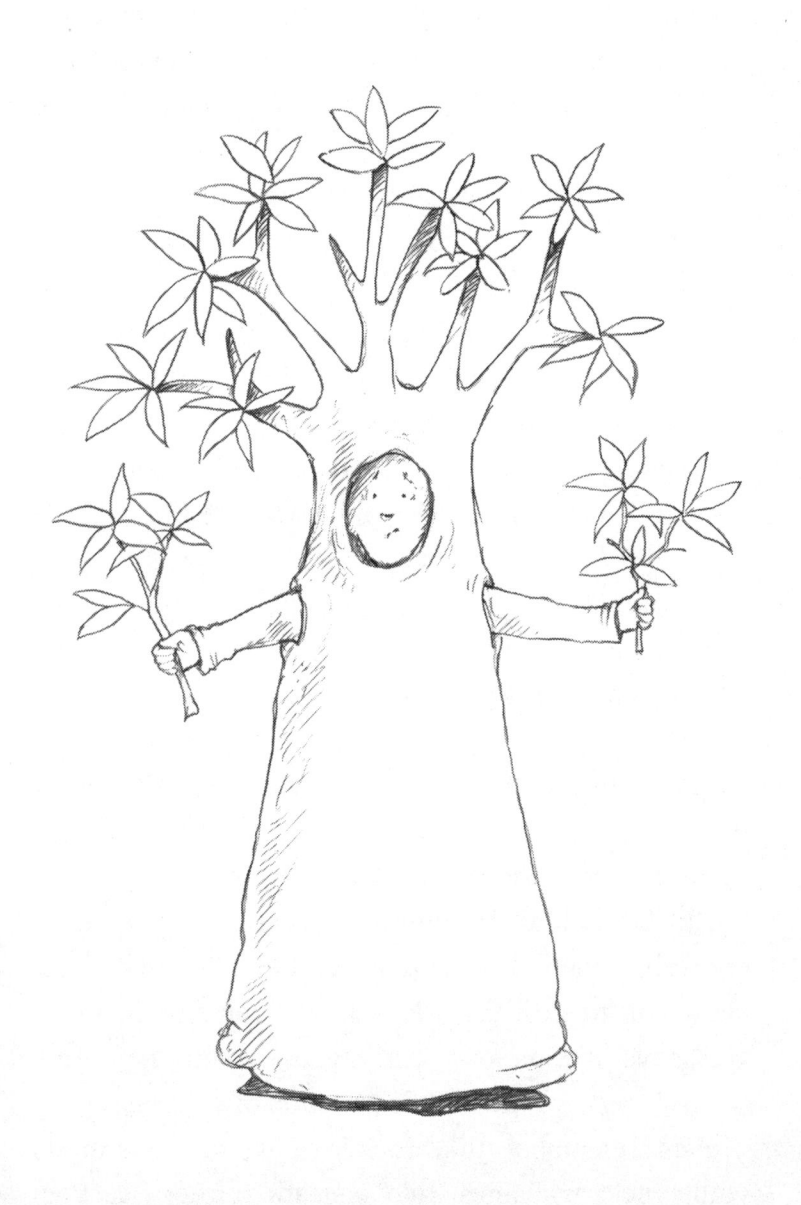

the side of their heads, so they can keep a look out over a wide area for any predators. But our eyes are on the front of our faces — like lions and dogs — which helps us to keep our prey in sight as we chase them.

Our faces tell roos and wallabies that we are a threat! So to disguise yourself, try to:

- wear a hat with a wide brim (this will disguise your hunter eyes and face shape);
- stand side-on, so that your shape looks more like a tree than a two-legged human. If you can, lift one leg up and support it on your knee, too, as a further disguise. I know this sounds uncomfortable — and it is! But it helps!
- stand perfectly still — and don't talk.

Don't be disappointed if your disguise doesn't always work, and the roos or wallabies bound away. Maybe there are other people about and they feel nervous.

But be patient. If you're lucky, after five minutes or so the roos will start to eat again. They may even allow you to slowly work your way towards them. If you have patience — and luck — you may find yourself right in the middle of a mob of feeding roos.

And remember that roos run if they're scared, while most wallabies hide instead. If they see you they may stay perfectly still and hope that you won't notice them. So if you stay perfectly still — and disguise yourself, too — you'll be able to get a good look at them.

If you hear the sound of thump, thump, thump, that means the roos or wallabies have seen or heard you and are racing off. Sadly though, by the time you hear this it's mostly too late to see them!

Fact

Many animals have characteristic smells. A mob of roos leave their scent in the air — and if the wind is in the right direction you'll know where they are — once you know what the scent of roos is like and you have got into the habit of smelling it.

Don't bother trying to disguise your smell. Roos and wallabies rely more on their eyes than their sense of smell to recognise danger. And any other scent you use to cover yours — like soap, or perfume — will smell strange to a roo anyway. (No, it *won't* think you're a flower if you wear a flowery scent!)

If you can, though, try to stand downwind. That way, the wind is blowing from them to you, and will blow your smell away from them.

The short story of walking with wallabies

Early every morning I go for a walk along our valley, then up the mountain. I usually see at least six wallabies along the way and a mob or two of roos. And mostly they don't bother to hop away till I'm so close I could almost touch them.

Some of the wallabies know me — the ones that live in our garden. But most of the others may not have seen me before.

Why don't they run away? Because I don't stare at them. I keep my head down and look at them out of the corner of my eye. I wear a hat with a big brim, too, which disguises my close-together 'predator' eyes. Grass eaters like roos have eyes on the side of their head. Animals like dogs, and humans, have eyes set close together. This signals danger to any grass eater. I don't stop or run, either, when I see a roo or wallaby but just keep walking steadily (usually slowly because it's a steep mountain). If I stopped, or began to hurry or made any sudden change in the way I moved at all, the wallabies would bound away at once.

I don't want to make any sign that might make them think, 'Help! This strange two-legged animal is hunting me. Run!'

11

Caring for orphan joeys

One day you're probably going to go past an orphaned joey — one who'll die, alone and helpless.

You may not even realise there is an orphaned joey nearby. You'll probably be in a car, speeding along the highway, and the baby will be on the side of the road, or even in the middle of the road, lying in its dead mother's pouch after she was hit by a car.

Thousands of roos, wombats and other native animals are killed on our roads every day — and many have babies in their pouches. Often the baby is killed, too. But sometimes the baby survives, as its mother's body has protected it, and her warmth helps keep the baby alive. Even if the mother has been lying by the side of the road all day the baby may still be alive.

If you go for a bushwalk, too, you may find a kangaroo or wallaby that's been killed by shooters, or one that has been attacked by dogs. It also may have a baby in its pouch that is still alive.

What to do with an orphaned or injured joey

If someone like you is able to rescue an injured joey, and take it to people who know how to care for orphaned joeys, it may grow up to be a happy wild kangaroo. Here's what to do if you find yourself in this situation.

Stop and investigate

If you're in a car, make sure it's safe to get out and to go up to the animal. You can't help anyone if you get run over! If the dead animal is in the middle of the road, be even more careful. If possible, have an adult flag down traffic to tell them to slow down. But again — only do this if it's safe and the cars can see anyone on the road in time to stop, even if they are speeding.

Now look in the pouch. If the baby is badly hurt it may be kinder to just leave it there — it's probably in shock and not feeling pain. If you try to move it, it will wake up, terrified. I know this is hard, but it can be the best thing to do.

If the baby doesn't have any fur, and its ears and eyes haven't formed properly yet, it won't have much chance of survival either, even if you can get it to an expert straight away. It may be worth rescuing the baby, but only if you know you can quickly get it to someone who knows just what to do.

Remove the unharmed and healthy joey

Before you lift the baby out from its mother's pouch, get a blanket or even your jacket to keep the baby warm, and decide on somewhere dark and quiet to put it — like in a box, or behind the front seat of your car, *not* on your lap.

Put on gloves, if you have them, or wrap your hands and arms in a towel or even a shirt — anything to make sure that the baby does not scratch or bite you. Touch the baby as little as possible.

I know you'd like someone to cuddle you and comfort you if you had just had your mum killed in a car accident, but a baby roo or wallaby will be scared of human voices and strange sounds.

Find expert help quickly

It isn't easy looking after a baby roo or wallaby. Many will die even when professionals look after them. It is illegal to look after native animals without a permit, too, and people who haven't been trained to look after baby animals can hurt them or even kill them, even when they're trying to be kind.

So leave the caring to people who have been trained!

Organisations like WIRES or Wildcare put up signs with their phone numbers along major roads. Or you

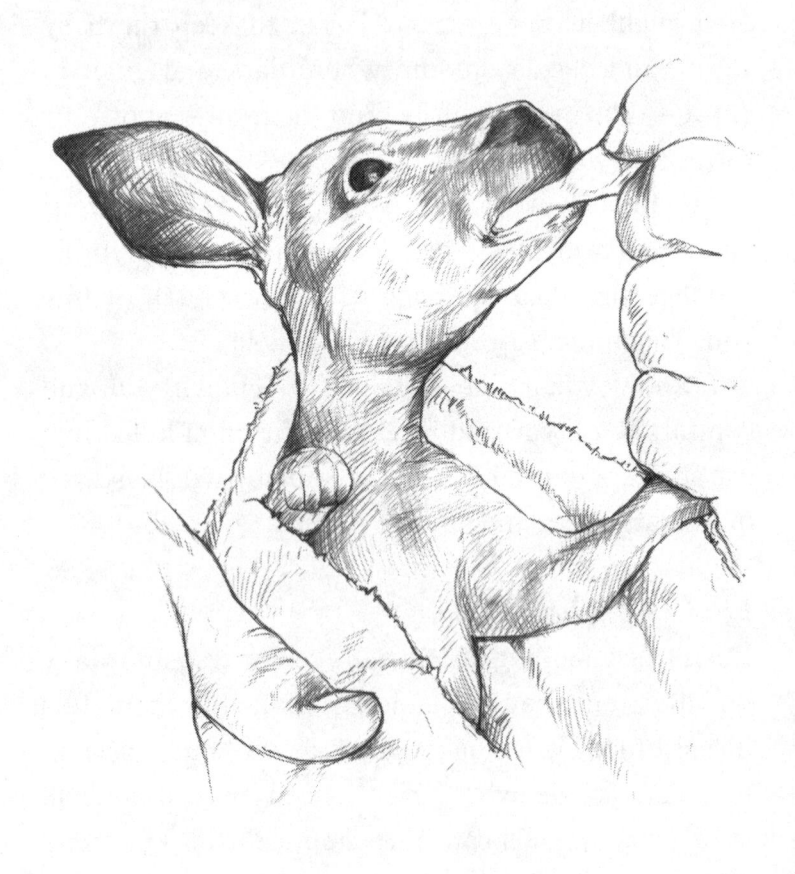

A young joey must be fed with a special marsupial teat

can look up their numbers in the phone book or on the Internet. Alternatively, ring any vet or national parks office and they will tell you who looks after orphaned joeys in your area. The police may also be able to help you find wildlife carers, though not in all places, and some local councils will help, too. You may need to make two or three calls, but you will find someone.

But say it's the middle of the night, or you are far away from a phone. What can you do until you can get the joey to an expert?

Keep the baby quiet on the way home. Don't have the radio on, don't yell or sing, and talk softly. Don't keep checking to see that the baby is all right.

When you get home, put the baby in the quietest room you have, like the spare room. But not the laundry, if possible, as that might be too cold. Keep any dogs well away, too, as their smell will terrify the baby.

Keep the baby warm. A pink joey (no fur) needs to be kept at a room temperature of between 32°C and 34°C. An electric blanket or a hot water bottle will help maintain this temperature. But make sure that the bottle is wrapped in a towel so that it doesn't burn the joey. Never put the joey directly onto an the electric blanket — put the blanket under other bed linen.

A very sudden change in temperature is bad for the joey too, so make sure that there are lots of layers of cloth between the baby and the source of heat so that it only slowly feels the extra heat. Use a thermometer if you can to make sure the temperature is right.

If the joey is older and has fur and it's a warm day or night, then all it needs is a bag or box with lots of soft, clean bed linen. A bag is best, because it resembles somewhere dark like its mum's pouch. But if you only have a box, drape some cloth over half of it. If it gets cold, use an electric blanket or hot water bottle. Older joeys need to be kept at between 28°C and 32°C.

It will be hard to give the joey up, even after a few hours. But looking after a joey is a lot of work — it needs to be fed every four hours, even at night, and each feed can take up to half an hour. It also needs to be cleaned, and an older joey needs to be watched over as it grazes.

But joeys need cuddling and playing with, too, so anyone who takes your joey may well like some extra help! You can also do courses with any of the wildlife organisations to teach you how to care for wildlife. Remember, even if you can't take on the care of an animal yourself, you can help others.

If you can't get the baby to expert care within a day, ask for advice from the carer you are talking to. Or if you can't speak to a carer for a while then offer the joey a little *boiled* water in a sterilised (boiled) bottle with a new marsupial teat — one specially made for roo and wallaby mouths (the ones for human babies are the wrong shape), which are available at many pharmacies.

But most importantly, just get the baby to expert care as soon as you can!

The story of Nuisance

Some neighbours brought Nuisance to me one Sunday afternoon. They'd found her hanging upside down from a barbed wire fence by one leg. They'd tried looking after her for a couple of days, but she wouldn't eat grass, or the bread and condensed milk they'd offered her. So, finally, they brought her to me. They'd heard I liked wild animals.

'We've called her Nuisance,' said one of them, 'because she is. She kept making a noise all night.'

Nuisance shivered in the cardboard box they'd brought her in. She was about a year old. Normally she'd have still been with her mum, living outside the pouch but still sticking her head in now and then for a drink.

I wondered what had happened. Had her mother been terrified? Had both she and her baby been running from a car or dogs or hunters?

I waited until the neighbours had left and it was quiet before I took a closer look at her. Nuisance cowered in her box, too weak to try to get away. Her foot was dislocated, deeply gashed and maggot ridden. She was dehydrated and terrified.

I didn't have a marsupial teat — a specially designed, very long and narrow teat for roos and wombats. (Their mouths are the wrong shape for the ones that human babies use.) I offered her boiled water in a spoon but she wouldn't take it, so I took her up to the vet. There were no volunteer groups back then to look after wildlife, but I'd helped look after joeys before.

The vet showed me how to clean the maggots out of her wound. He injected her with antibiotics, and I went and bought the right teats and milk formula to feed her — roos and wallabies get sick if you feed them cow's milk. I took her home, and tried to feed her again.

She spent the rest of that day shivering, panting in terror at the sight of a human — she made small growls at the back of her throat and stared with wide dark eyes. She still wouldn't drink.

I made her a pouch from a hessian bag and soft blankets, with a rope to hang it from a chair. She couldn't walk to get into it, so I lifted her instead.

The second day she accepted my hands stroking her, scratching her. She sucked water from my fingers. When I offered her the bottle again she drank a little. On the third day I saw her watching me as I ate a piece of watermelon. I offered her a tiny piece. She took it delicately and held it carefully in both paws. The juice ran down her chin and chest and she scratched the dribbles absentmindedly.

Like other young roos, wallabies and wombats, Nuisance grew attached to humans very quickly. By the fourth day she liked to be cuddled, as though she was in a pouch. She cried if I left her, so I started to carry her pouch with me all the time, even into the bathroom.

Her foot hurt her. The wound was deeper than I'd first thought. I took her back to the vet to get it re-dressed. Nuisance woke every hour or so all through that night. I'd feed her, but it was mostly comfort she wanted, like anyone in pain. I'd stroke her head or scratch her tummy. She'd stretch back in ecstasy and scratch with her hands too, leaning on her tail to avoid putting weight on her foot.

Every evening I took her outside, to lie on the grass and to nibble a bit. But even then the flies buzzed round. I made a sort of tent from mosquito net to put over her.

But her foot got fly blown again anyway, and her anus, though her droppings were firm and she seemed healthy. It should have warned me. But she seemed to be getting better. She was finally eating well, chewing bits of apple and demanding the best, greenest grass — no couch grass or wallaby grass, but the nice thick kikuyu grass at a neighbour's. I took her down there every evening to graze, and picked more to feed her when we got home, but she still liked her bottle.

She started to get fatter too. Her ribs no longer seemed sharp and fragile beneath her fur. She played with dangled bits of wool; embraced my wrist and rubbed her face along my hand. She even started to bound a few steps about the garden. Her foot looked like it was almost healed.

I thought she was going to be fine.

Then one morning she seemed quiet. I thought it might be the heat. I kept her indoors in the cool stone bedroom. She fussed over her foot all morning. I looked at it. You could hardly see the wound in the fur now. By afternoon she was writhing, arching back in pain. I inspected her foot again. It was swollen and seemed to pulsate. She let me look at it. Her eyes were duller and her coat rough.

I squeezed around the scab. It broke. Maggots oozed out. The wound smelled sour. I cleaned it, as the vet had shown me, as I'd been doing several times a day. I thought of the medieval superstition that maggots generated from nowhere, from evil humours. There seemed no way a fly could have reached her.

I took her to the vet, a hot trip in the hot truck. She kept licking her paws but refused a bottle, even bits of watermelon, but would take a little water dripped from my fingers.

The vet wasn't there. He was down the coast. He'd be back late that night, but Nuisance died that afternoon.

The vet told me later she had gangrene. He'd thought it might happen. The wound was too deep and her foot had been badly damaged when she hung from the fence, so that there wasn't enough blood supply to it. But he'd thought that there wasn't much use telling me he didn't think she was going to live. He thought I'd have tried to help her, anyway. He was right. And there was nothing else either of us could have done.

But I felt I'd betrayed her. She had trusted me to look after her, and I had let her down. It was hard to even look at the roos grazing up on the hill. I'd see the young ones with their mothers and remember Nuisance.

It was another three years before I could bring myself to look after another kangaroo.

12

Protecting our roos and wallabies

Over the past two hundred years humans have taken most of the land where kangaroos and wallabies lived for 1 them when they search for food along the side of our roads — often the only land that isn't eaten out by sheep and cattle.

We've introduced feral rabbits, camels and goats that eat their grass and shrubs. We've brought foxes and packs of wild dogs that hunt them. Bushfires burn their food (most bushfires are started by people, not lightning). These animals are threatened because of us.

Unlike many wild animals, roos and wallabies aren't dangerous. We should be able to all share the world together. And there are ways we can — if enough people care.

Roos on the road

Drivers who travel a lot outside the city need to learn how to avoid hitting roos, because often the only food around for roos and wallabies is along the roadside. Learn to look at the edges of the road. Most city drivers focus mostly on the road ahead, which is what you have to do if you drive in traffic. But bush drivers learn to keep a watch on the sides of the road.

Drivers should go especially slowly in the early evening and early morning, when animals are moving to their feeding areas.

Look at what the roos or wallabies are doing. A roo on all fours is eating. A roo standing straight up, its ears twitching, is alarmed, and may well leap very fast to get away from danger — your car. Unfortunately, a kangaroo is just as likely to panic and bound across the road as it is to turn and leap into the bush away from the road. If a driver sees a roo standing straight up, then they need to slow right down to avoid a roo who is trying to get away fast.

Finally, drivers shouldn't drive when they're tired, and can't react quickly. (This may save their life, too, as well as roos and wallabies.)

Living with roos on farms

Roos and wallabies eat grass — and some farmers feel every blade of grass belongs to their sheep or cattle.

Roo meat is a cheap way to feed the dogs, too. But a good population of roos will help the land. In bad drought years, the grass seeds in their dung can survive for decades, and will grow into pasture when the rain comes again. Farmers with roos and wallabies on their land may find that their farms recover after drought much faster than land that only has sheep or cattle. The micro-organisms in roo and wallaby dung will help keep soil creatures called nematodes alive, too, which in turn will help keep plague grasshoppers under control. Wallabies also help control woody weeds.

Often farmers think they have far more roos or wallabies than there really are, because in droughts they all crowd around creeks or dams for water or in paddocks of lucerne or wheat for food, or along the sides of roads where there is a little green grass. But there are *never* plagues of roos or wallabies in a drought. All those roos are just starving ones coming from somewhere else. The only time roos may need to be culled is a dry time after several really good years of lush grass, when suddenly there isn't enough grass to feed everyone anymore. And wallabies very rarely need to be culled at all.

Roos are often blamed for rabbit damage. A paddock will be eaten to the ground and the farmer will blame the roos grazing there in the dusk instead of the rabbits that come out after the farmer has gone to bed. Rabbit dung is also more likely to foul dams than roo droppings. But roos are bigger than rabbits — and the farmer sees the roos and doesn't see the bunnies.

Roos can, in fact, help maintain improved pastures — because they much prefer native pasture in most cases, and will munch species that might otherwise compete with the introduced pasture grasses.

In our barbed-wire-loving district you often see roos with their feet caught in barbed wire, wallabies with ripped tails, possums who've been tangled. If fences are in good order — taut and well strained — you don't need barbed wire.

Keeping a roo as a pet

Don't! Kangaroos are wild animals and you have to have a permit to look after one if it's injured or orphaned. And it's not fair to keep a roo in a small area. Roos need to be able to bound over tens of kilometres. But if you move to the bush and join one of the societies that care for injured roos, then the roos you care for can go free on your property when they grow up or get better. And for a while they may come back to say 'hi'.

Some schools near bushland even have wild roos eating their grass. But a suburban school probably couldn't get a permit to look after orphaned animals — they'd be in too much danger from cars and dogs.

Anyone who does care for hurt or baby wild animals has to be very careful to keep the animal wild — not get it too used to humans — so it can go back to the bush safely.

Sometimes hand-reared joeys chase cars or follow walkers with dogs because they want to have fun with humans again. And the dogs or cars can kill them. Wild animals deserve the chance to be free.

There's a wallaby in my garden

Roos don't damage gardens — they just tread on them a bit. But wallabies do eat gardens. They also pull down branches, breaking them or even splitting young trees in half.

We have a four-hectare garden and about six hundred fruit trees. And we have a lot of wallabies and they are allowed to wander where they like.

So why isn't our garden eaten by wallabies? Because over the past few decades I've worked out how I can still have my garden and the wallabies can still have an interesting breakfast.

We put netting 'guards' over our young trees. We also prune off the lower branches. When the trees are too tall for the wallabies to reach we pull off the guards and use them on another tree. Simple.

I surround some young trees with plants, like tall dahlias, that wallabies don't like. They don't bother going through the hedges of dahlias to find the young apple trees.

We grow the vegies wallabies really adore in an area called 'The Tiger Pen', because it looks like we've put up strong fences to keep tigers in. I grow lettuce, carrots, celery, corn and other green vegetables there.

But mostly, wallabies don't like tomatoes, eggplant, asparagus, pumpkin, zucchini, melons, cucumbers, artichokes, capsicum and chillies, so I grow these where the wallabies can nose around and eat the weeds from between the plants.

I grow big rambling roses up our trees, where the wallabies can't reach them. (Rambling roses are easy to grow, too, and birds love to nest in them. And they are so big that we have hundreds of thousands of roses in spring.)

I grow lots of flowers, too, that wallabies don't like — most bulbs like daffodils and tulips, gladioli and freesias; most 'rhizome' plants with long roots like ginger lilies and iris; and agapanthus or any of the sage family. There are hundreds of these with glorious flowers, and members of the sage family survive the worst droughts, too. Wallabies don't eat most natives shrubs once they're more than a year old or so, because they have tough leaves, not nice tender ones to nibble. In fact, look for tough-leafed, or fragrant-leafed plants. Protect them for a year or two, then the wallabies will mostly leave them alone. (*See also* jackiefrench.com for more plants wallabies don't like.)

In bad drought years wallabies eat just about everything. But these very bad times only last a few months. (Although droughts can go on for ten or more years, the really bad periods don't last that long.) When a bit of rain returns wallabies will go back to their normal diet. And your garden will grow back — often all the better for being pruned by the wallabies.

> ### Fact
> Wallabies often follow the scent of wombats to crawl through the holes they make under a fence. If you want to exclude wallabies from an area that wombats travel through put in a heavy wombat 'gate' — wire with a heavy metal or wood edge. Wombats will push through a heavy gate but wallabies can't. Or push a concrete pipe into the hole under the fence. The wombat will walk down the pipe, but the wallaby won't.

What you can do to help preserve wildlife

- Write to your Member of Parliament asking for more national parks — and for money for more park rangers to fight fires properly, to control feral animals and to patrol to stop shooters.
- Raise money for organisations like the Bush Heritage Fund to help buy back privately owned land for native animals.
- Ask adults to slow down when driving at night when roos and wallabies are feeding.
- Help keep your dog in at night, and help train them to come to you when they're called.

- Join organisations that care for injured and orphaned wildlife and help adult carers to look after them.
- Keep an eye out for suspicious-looking people who light bushfires. Watch out for kids who are inclined to play with matches and tell a sensible adult! If you see anyone lighting a fire, call 000.
- Check the pouches of female roos and wallabies that have been hit by cars, in case there are orphaned babies who are still alive.
- Remember, kids, that this is your world! Adults are just looking after it for you. If you think they're doing a bad job, tell them! Write letters to your local paper and explain what you would do to make it better.
- Most of all, visit the bush. Walk, sit and watch the animals. Learn to love them. Learn the incredible joy of being with them, of understanding animals who are truly wild. The more we love our wildlife, the more we'll fight to help them survive.

The story of the dancing kangaroo

Once upon a time there was a kangaroo called Fuchsia. Her mother had been shot but Fuchsia had survived, and in a roundabout way she ended up with us.

This was a long time ago, down in the valley (where I live now with my young son in what was basically a machinery shed, with gas lights instead of electric power, and a bathroom with a roof but no windows.

We were broke but it was a magical time. It rained a lot that year and the creek gurgled and the grass grew, and there was fruit on the trees and vegies in the garden.

And then Fuchsia arrived.

Her adopted human mother, Mary, was struggling to look after a pair of young Swampies, guzzling and tearing up the furniture. It was too much to look after Fuchsia too, especially now that she was getting bigger and needed to go for two walks a day and play outdoors. It's hard to give a joey enough exercise in the suburbs when there are dogs about.

Fuchsia would be able to bounce around our garden. And when she was ready she could hop off into the bush.

'She's the sweetest roo I've ever looked after,' said Mary. 'You'll love her.'

She was right.

My son loved her, too. A three-year-old and a joey like doing much the same things. They raced each other down the orchard. Fuchsia

would always win, but she was very polite about waiting for him.

The three of us went for a walk every dusk, that gentle time when the sun is behind the ridges and the animals come out to drink. Well, I walked and my son ran and Fuchsia jumped in great bounding circles around us.

Fuchsia soon learned where all the gates were and the wombat holes under the fences; and how you waited for one to be opened for you and wriggled through the other. But she never did learn not to jump on my bed.

Then one night, after the three of us came in from our evening walk, I put Peter Combe's 'Newspaper Mama' tape on for my son to dance to while I made dinner. And when I looked around the two of them were dancing — boy and kangaroo. Fuchsia danced across the kitchen. She danced over the chairs. She danced over my son too.

Every time I put a tape on after that, Fuchsia danced — wonderful leaping dances. Sometimes it was hard to concentrate on cooking, and not just watch the boy and the dancing kangaroo.

Fuchsia was getting bigger now. Before, she'd sleep most of the time, coming out to play in the late afternoon. But now she was awake most of the night, bouncing around the kitchen. I left piles of grass for her to eat, under the chairs or behind the sofa, so she could have fun hunting them out.

By the time she was sixteen months old she spent every night outside. But she still liked her bottle in the morning.

I'd wake up to the thundering of kangaroo feet as she did six wake-up-the-inhabitants circuits of the house. Then she'd be at the bedroom door. 'Eeeaaaarrr!' A noise that meant anything from 'Feed me' to 'Scratch my ears', a literal translation probably being, 'Here I am'.

You can't sleep with a kangaroo bleating at the door. She was offended if I didn't open the door at once.

And then . . .

I still shiver when I think of it. In those days, when my son went to preschool, I wrote at a friend's house up in town, with Fuchsia in her basket and friend's dog Imma sitting on my feet. Imma was one of the gentlest, best-trained dogs I have ever known, half black lab and half Alsatian. Imma would sniff at Fuchsia's basket but never even growl.

But one day my friend and Imma joined us for our evening walk. Something, an owl maybe, spooked Fuchsia, so she ran. The running must have stirred a distant instinct because suddenly Imma ran too, and grabbed Fuschia by the throat.

My son was screaming and I was crying as we pulled Imma's jaws apart. I had seen a wallaby injured like that just the year before — only two puncture wounds, but the wallaby's windpipe had been pierced. She died soon after.

I tried to lift Fuchsia to see how badly she'd been hurt. But she ran. I was an enemy now. I smelled of dog.

I never held Fuchsia again. I never saw her, either. Not really. Not to say, yes, that's the kangaroo I know.

But about a year later, driving my son back from preschool, I stopped to open the farm gate. The tape was blaring out 'Newspaper Mama' and my son was singing, and up on the hill near the apricot trees was a mob of roos. As we watched, one of them broke away from the others.

And she began to dance.

She danced around the apricot trees. She danced around the other roos.

And every night after that as I've passed the roos on the hill I've wondered if maybe I'll see them dancing too, and known that nothing has ever given me so much joy as sharing my life with animals.

Roo phrases

Australians use many, many phrases with roo or wallaby in them.

I'm a kangarooster.
I live in Australia.

Do you have kangaroo paws in your garden?
You might have! No, not the hopping sort — kangaroo paws are attractive flowers from Western Australia. We also grow kangaroo apples — a native solanum with pretty purple berries.

We put a roo bar on the ute.
We put a bull bar on the ute — a thick metal frame to stop the car being dented if it hits a kangaroo.

They tried him in a kangaroo court.
A kangaroo court is one where you won't get a fair trial. It probably comes from the early colonial days when soldiers of the New South Wales Corps were in charge of trials — and made sure that their mates were always innocent and their enemies always guilty.

She lives somewhere out past the kangaroo fence.
A kangaroo fence is one built to keep kangaroos out. It's usually made of odd bits of wood, rather than neat posts and netting. Someone who lives west of 'the fence' lives in the 'outback'.

The soldier had a kangaroo feather in his hat.
In the First World War members of the Australian Light Horse wore a plume of Emu feathers in their hats — and as a joke they were called 'kangaroo feathers'.

The car gave a kangaroo hop.
The car gave a jerk.

When we went to England we stayed in Kangaroo Valley.

Earls Court, a suburb in London, has been called Kangaroo Valley since the 1940s because so many young travelling Australians stay there.

We flew the kangaroo route to London.

The kangaroo route was the route between Australia and London that Qantas, whose logo is a flying kangaroo, made commercially viable in the 1940s and on which it had a monopoly until relatively recently.

The kangaroo grass was turning red up on the hill.

Kangaroo grass is a native grass, *Themeda triandra*. It turns rusty red in autumn.

He had kangaroos in his top paddock . . .
He was bonkers or very silly.

I was badly bitten by kangaroo flies.

A kangaroo fly is a kangaroo 'bot' fly — an extremely annoying, small brown fly.

The toilets looked filthy so I kangaroo hopped the seat.

A kangaroo hop is crouching with your feet up on the toilet seat to go to the toilet.

Roo and wallaby jokes

Why did the kangaroo cross the road?
He'd lost his jumper.

What's it like being a wallaby?
Well, it has its ups and downs.

What do you call a kangaroo who tells a naughty joke?
Roo-d.

*What do you say to a kangaroo who's ten years old **today**?*
Hoppy birthday.

What has green hair, a nose stud and goes boing, boing?
Spiky the punk kangaroo.

What don't you give a kangaroo for Christmas?
A pogo stick.

What did the teacher tell the bad wallaby?
You broke the roo–ls!

How can you tell if a kangaroo's been in the fridge?
There are tail prints in the butter.

What do wallabies do when they meet the Queen of England?
Bow-nce.

Why did the kangaroo jump in the dunny?
It wanted to see the bottom.

What sort of animal has a long tail and stinks?
A kanga-poo.

What fruit is like a kangaroo's sore foot?
A paw-paw (poor paw).

Where do wallabies keep their mobile phones?
In their pouch.

What sort of bee has a tail?
A wallaby. (Wally bee)

Who's the most royal marsupial?
A kingaroo.

What do you call a kangaroo who jumps into a mud puddle?
A kanga-gooey.

What else do you call a kangaroo who jumps into a mud puddle?
Wet.

What sort of animal goes hop, hop, hop-a-doodle doo?
A kangarooster.

What do you call a wallaby who eats all the sweets?
A lollyby.

Why was the kangaroo angry with her joey?
He didn't take his soccer boots off before he went to bed.

What's blue and goes hop, shiver, hop?
A kangaroo in your ice-cream.

What's red and goes flip-flop-hop, flip-flop-hop?
A sunburnt kangaroo in a pair of thongs.

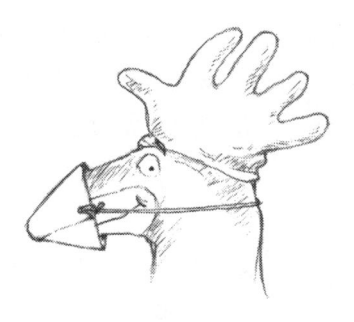

What sort of chicken doesn't lay eggs?
A roo-ster.

Mummy, mummy, why do the other kids call me a kangaroo?
Shut up and get back in your pouch.

What do you get if you cross a sheep and a wallaby?
A woolly jumper.

What's the worst thing about being a joey in a pouch?
There's no room to read in bed!

What sport do marsupials play?
Australian Roo-ls.

Mummy, mummy, why do the other kids call me a wallaby?
Just finish eating your grass and do your homework!

What do you call a hundred-year-old kangaroo?
A roo-in.

What do you call 1,000 kangaroos sitting on your house?
Your roo-f.

What do you call a giant prehistoric kangaroo with fangs?
Sir.

Who's Who of Wallabies and Roos

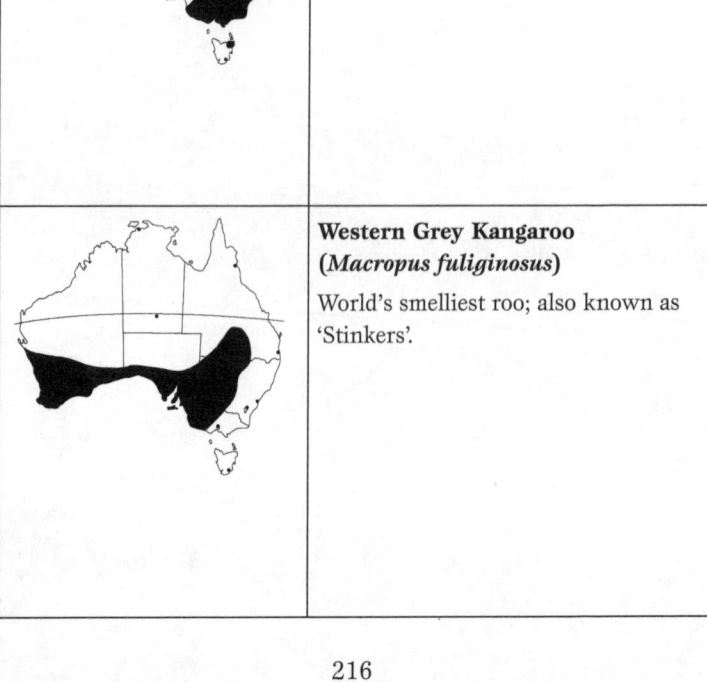

Found	Name and Star Quality
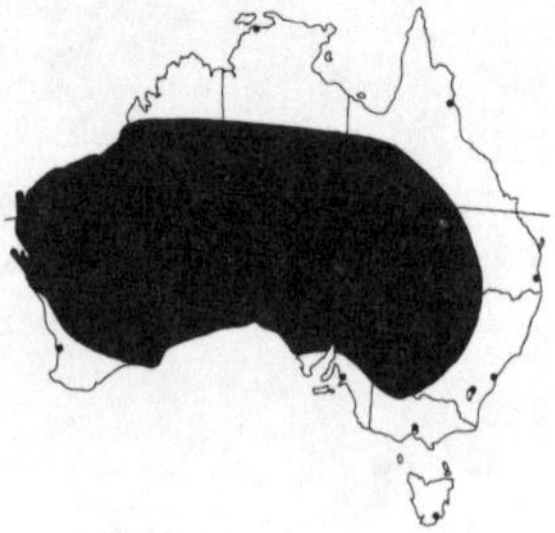	**Red Kangaroo** (*Macropus rufus*) World's biggest roo; has lots of muscle power.
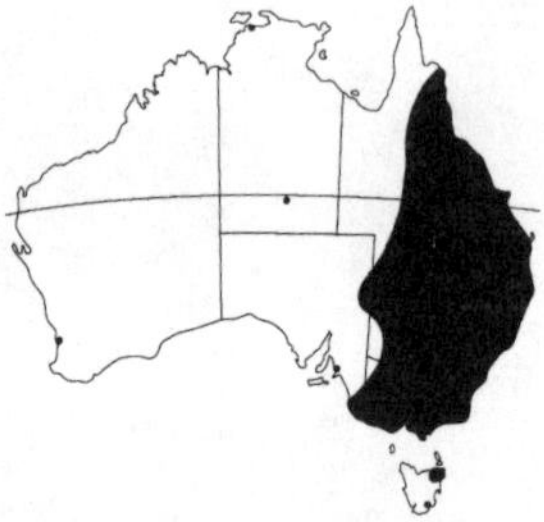	**Eastern Grey Kangaroo** (*Macropus giganteus*) World's most popular roo; appears on Australia's coat of arms.
	Western Grey Kangaroo (*Macropus fuliginosus*) World's smelliest roo; also known as 'Stinkers'.

Looks	Habits
Stands 2 m; weighs 90 kg; tail length up to 1m; long squarish muzzle and long ears; male is rusty colour; female is soft bluish grey with white front.	Lives in mob ranging from one 'boss' male with three or four females and joeys to mob of 400 with many big males; usually found near waterholes at dusk or dawn; mob rests in shade during the day. Mostly eats grass.
Stands about 2.5 m; weighs up to 70 kg; taller, more delicate-looking than Red. Has soft woolly fur, big pointed ears and furry grey-brown muzzle — although bare around its nostrils. Female is smaller than the male.	Lives in mob with big 'boss' male; mobs usually smaller than Red mobs; often found resting in shade of trees during the day, or feeding at dusk and dawn; will sometimes graze in moonlight. Mostly eats grass; doesn't browse on other plants, even when very hungry.
Stands 1–2.25 m; weighs up to 55 kg; a bit smaller than both Red and Eastern; has brown coat and whiskers on its nose.	Lives in mob; usually found resting in shade of trees during the day, or feeding at dusk and dawn; will sometimes graze in moonlight. Mostly eat grass.

Found	Name and Star Quality
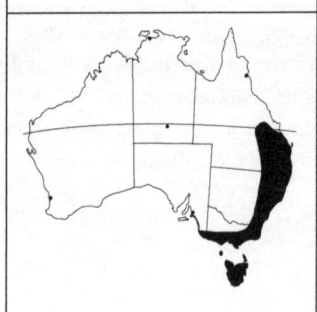	**Red-necked Wallaby** (***Macropus rufogriseus***) (a.k.a. Bennett's Wallaby or Kangaroo in Tasmania) Long, soft grey and red fur. Introduced to New Zealand in nineteenth century and has since become a pest.
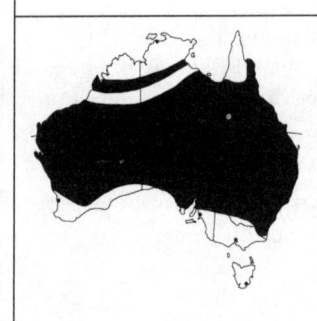	**Wallaroo or Euro** (**various *Macropus* species**) Big, black bare nose!
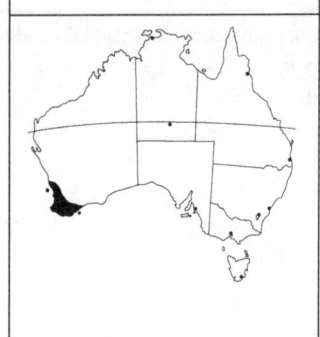	**Quokka** (***Setonix brachyurus***) (a.k.a. Short-tailed Wallaby) Extremely cute and pretty; has the shortest feet of any roo or wallaby; studied by medical research for muscular dystrophy as they suffer from same disease.

Looks	Habits
Mainland Red-neck stands 77–85 cm; tail slightly shorter than body; Tasmanian Red-neck very slightly smaller; is blunt nosed; beautifully fluffy with reddish fur on top and grey below.	Lives mostly by itself, but joins mob to eat; usually found grazing out in open, especially on late winter afternoons. Likes to eat nice short, soft green grass; loves lush introduced grasses like kikuyu.
Stands 1.5–1.75 m; weighs 18–45 kg. Smaller than kangaroo, more graceful and larger than wallaby; short roo-like fur and long, graceful, roo-like bound.	Common and Black Wallaroo lives by itself, not in a mob; the Antilopene Wallaroo lives in mob of three to thirty. Found on rocky hills, sheltering in caves and sunbaking on rock ledges. Eats grasses and shrubs; can survive on poor dry grass.
Stands 80 cm; weighs 2.7–4.2 kg; long, coarse grey fur; short, stiff tail; ears more rounded than other wallabies and skull and teeth are different; has rapid hop and leap, rather than bound and lope.	Mostly found on Rottnest Island; small groups on mainland in WA. Lives in mob of twenty-five to 250; sleeps in the shade during the day; usually found at water 'soaks' at dusk. Eats leaves and bark from small shrubs, grass, just about any plant around, including pigface.

Found	Name and Star Quality
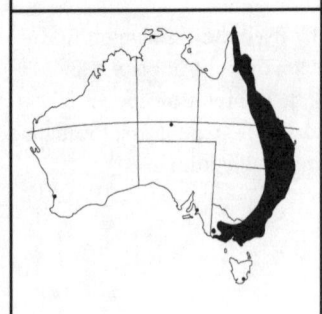	**Swamp Wallaby** (*Wallabia bicolor*) (a.k.a. Black-tailed Wallaby, Black Wallaby, Stinkers, Fern Wallaby) Known as gourmet wallaby; can sit back on bum and tail, not just crouch on legs.
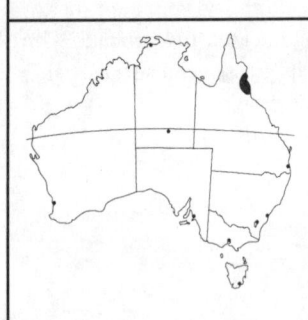	**Lumholtz's Tree-kangaroo** (*Dendrolagus lumholtzi*) Has the biggest tummy, for its size, of any roo, allowing more time for leaves to be digested.
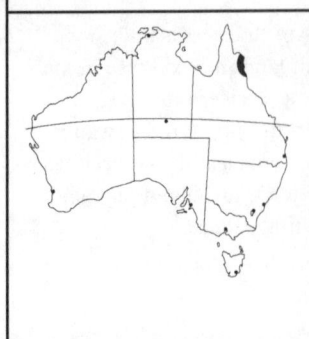	**Bennett's Tree-kangaroo** (*Dendrolagus bennettianus*) Considered a delicacy by indigenous people in the late nineteenth century.

Looks	Habits
Stands 65–75 cm; weighs 12–20 kg; tail about same length as body; mostly black on top, greyish on sides and rusty colour underneath; pale face and dark areas around eyes. Swampies can vary a lot in colour; some have white tips on tails, some mostly black, others with more reddish fur on tummies and some with lighter fawn faces.	Lives mostly by itself. Most common and widespread wallaby. Usually found feeding in grassy clearings at dawn or dusk. Eats young shrubs, grasses, leaves, fruit, anything in human garbage or compost bins; sometimes even meat (which makes them pong badly).
Stands 48–59 cm; weighs 3.7–7 kg; tail is longer than body; sooty coloured on top with a pale tummy and arms, black face with a pale band across forehead and down each side and on hands and feet.	Lives mostly in trees by itself; male often growls at and fights other males, especially if a female nearby. To spot one be very quiet, use a torch at night, or look up at trees during the day; sometimes wildlife tours may be able to show you one. Eats rainforest leaves, tree shoots and fruit; also feeds in veggie gardens.
Stands 50–65 cm; weighs 13 kg; tail is much longer than its body and has a black end.	Lives mostly in trees by itself; male often growls at and fights other males, especially if a female nearby. To spot one be very quiet, use a torch at night, or look up at trees during the day; sometimes wildlife tours may be able to show you one. Eats rainforest leaves, tree shoots and fruit; also feeds in veggie gardens.

Found	Name and Star Quality
	Hare-wallaby (*Lagorchestes* **species**) Only wallaby that makes grass tunnels; loses less water than any other mammal its size.
	Nailtail Wallaby (*Onychogalea* **species**) A 3-mm horny spur at end of its tail allows it to take off incredibly quickly, going from standing to full bound in a second; used to be called a 'flashjack' for its sudden burst of speed.
	Warabi Wallaby (*Petrogale burbidgei*) Smallest wallaby of all.

Looks	Habits
Stands 4–4.7 cm; weighs 1.5–4.5 kg; tail is as long as its body; pale brown on top with white-tipped hair; pale underparts, with rusty rings around the eyes; looks more like a European hare than a wallaby, apart from back legs.	Lives mostly by itself in open forests, shrublands or grasslands. Hare-wallaby is so tiny it's fair game for dogs, feral cats and foxes, but sometimes joins a small group to feed; hides behind tufts of grass like a hare. It makes tunnels in spinifex clumps and hides there during heat of the day. Eats young shrubs and spinifex tips, very occasionally grass. Spectacled Hare-wallaby doesn't drink at all, so is perfectly adapted to living in hot dry places.
Stands 30–70 cm; tail is longer than its body; distinctive black and white stripes on head and body; small, delicate-looking.	Mostly lives by itself in semi-arid areas where dense acacia shrubland and grassy woodland meet; occasionally five or six graze together; hides from danger in hollow logs or under bushes or lies flat in long grass or by fences; female sometimes leaves young under bushes when out grazing; rests during the day under a bush or tree; comes out to graze at night. Eats leaves, pigweed, flowers and grasses.
Stands 1 m tall; weighs 1 kg.	Lives in rocky areas in the remote parts of Kimberleys; very rare to spot; little known about species, as only described for the first time late last century. Probably eats native grasses, tussocks and leaves.

Found	Name and Star Quality
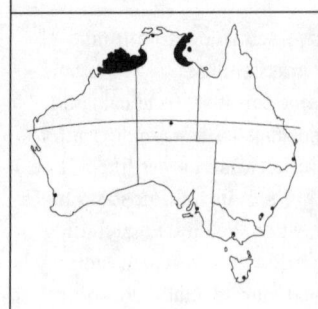	**Nabarlek** (*Petrogale concinna*) Thought to be the smallest Rock Wallaby, until discovery of Warabi.
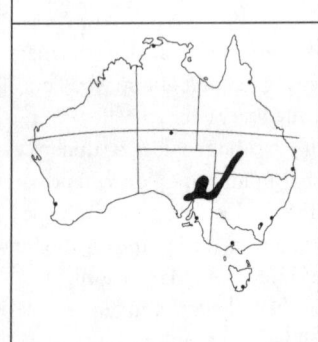	**Yellow-footed Rock Wallaby** (*Petrogale xanthopus*) Most beautifully coloured of all marsupials.
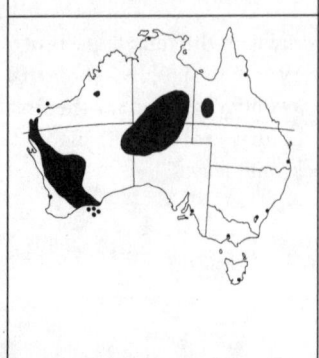	**Black-footed Rock Wallaby** (*Petrogale lateralis*) Known for its . . . black feet.

Looks	Habits
Stands 22–35 cm tall; weighs 1–1.7 kg; tail is about half as long as its body; tail has black brushy tip; fluffy, pale grey–white tummy and fawny rusty colour on top; dark stripe between ears.	Lives mostly by itself except mother with joey; if lucky, can be spotted at dawn or dusk when it comes down to drink; may leave droppings or fur on ledges or in small caves. Eats grass, new shoots, weeds and fruit. Rock Wallabies used to thrive throughout large areas of Australia, now only survive in a few isolated rocky outcrops in NSW, SA and Qld.
Stands 4.8–6.6 m; weighs 6–7 kg; tail slightly longer than body; grey on top with startlingly white tummy and stripes, reddish arms and legs, red-and-brown striped tail and white stripe on face and ears; feet are brownish yellow fading to red along legs.	Lives mostly by itself except mother with joey; if lucky, can be spotted at dawn or dusk when it comes down to drink; may leave droppings or fur on ledges or in small caves. Eats grass, new shoots, weeds and fruit. Rock Wallabies used to thrive throughout large areas of Australia, now only survive in a few isolated rocky outcrops in NSW, SA and Qld.
Stands up to 47 cm; weighs up to 3.5 kg; brownish-grey tail with black tip, up to 52 cm long; dark grey–brown with a thick, woolly coat; distinct white cheek stripe and dark brown to black stripe running from ears down beyond shoulders.	Lives mostly by itself except mother with joey; if lucky, can be spotted at dawn or dusk when it comes down to drink; may leave droppings or fur on ledges or in small caves. Eats grass, new shoots, weeds and fruit. Rock Wallabies used to thrive throughout large areas of Australia, now only survive in a few isolated rocky outcrops in NSW, SA and Qld.

Found	Name and Star Quality
	Proserpine Rock Wallaby (*Petrogale persephone*) Scientists only identified it as a separate species of wallaby in 1976.
	Brush-tailed Rock Wallaby (*Petrogale penicillata*) Has a distinct brush at the end of its tail.
	Pademelon (*Thylogale stigmatica*) (*T. thetis*) (*T. billardierii*) There are three species in Australia: Red-legged which can sit back on base of its tail, Red-necked and Tasmanian Pademelon; Pademelons can also 'talk' to each other.

Looks	Habits
Standss 52–64 cm; weighs 5–8 kg; shy and delicate-looking.	Lives mostly by itself except mother with joey; if lucky, can be spotted at dawn or dusk when it comes down to drink; may leave droppings or fur on ledges or in small caves. Eats grass, new shoots, weeds and fruit. Rock Wallabies used to thrive throughout large areas of Australia, now only survive in a few isolated rocky outcrops in NSW, SA and Qld.
Stands 4.5–5.8 m tall; weighs 5.5–7.8 kg; tail a bit longer than its body; dull brown on top and reddish near tail.	Lives mostly by itself except mother with joey; if lucky, can be spotted at dawn or dusk when it comes down to drink; may leave droppings or fur on ledges or in small caves. Eats grass, new shoots, weeds and fruit. Rock Wallabies used to thrive throughout large areas of Australia, now only survive in a few isolated rocky outcrops in NSW, SA and Qld.
Stands 60–120 cm; weighs 2.5–12 kg; small, cute wallaby.	Lives in large groups; often find groups feeding on grassy areas near rainforests; has a range of noises used for communication — a series of clicks, growls, hisses and chucking sounds; may also thump ground with feet to warn of danger. Makes runways through the dense vegetation. Red-legged Pademelons mostly eat leaves, but like fruit; Tasmanian and Red-necked Pademelons like short green grass, but will eat leaves and shoots.

Found	Name and Star Quality
	**Black-striped Wallaby** (*Macropus dorsalis*) One of the most colourful wallabies.
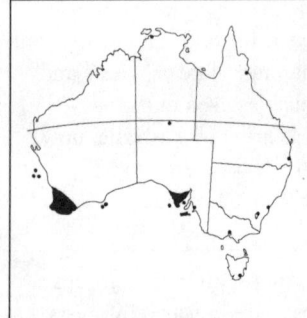	**Tammar Wallaby** (*Macropus eugenii*) One of the smallest and cutest wallabies; incredibly soft fur, Aboriginal people used to make cloaks with it; the first roos seen by European explorers. Tammars on Houtman Abrolhos islands off WA can survive by drinking sea water if no fresh water available.
	**Western Brush Wallaby** (*Macropus irma*) (a.k.a. Black-gloved Wallaby) Only wallaby to wear black gloves.

Looks	Habits
Stands 1.1–1.5 m; male weighs up to 20 kg; female about 6–7 kg; tail is about half the length of its body; rusty-red patches on shoulders, arms and upper legs and white stripes on hips and cheeks, black stripe down centre of grey–brown back.	Lives in mobs of about twenty; is shy and stays near bushes where it can hide; shelters during the day, comes out at dusk to feed; uses same track to get to grassy clearings each day, so usually can find them by following 'wallaby trails'. Logging and land clearing for farms has meant the groups are too far apart to be able to breed with each other, so they're becoming endangered.
Stands 52–68 cm; weighs 4–7.5 kg; a tail slightly shorter than its body; dark grey–brown back, pale grey–brown tummy and reddish sides and legs; rounded ears; short, sweet furry face that's paler on the cheeks and dark on top.	Lives on the islands off WA and SA, like Kangaroo Island, where there are no foxes; doesn't form mob but is sweet-natured, kind little wallaby that doesn't mind living near other Tammars; usually found in open grassy areas at dusk; eats tussocks, or leaves and weeds if no grass around.
Weighs about 7–9 kg; tall, graceful wallaby standing at about 1.2 m; hands, feet, tips of ears and end of tail are black, with a crest of black hair on tail; white stripe on face, rest of fur is grey, so black really stands out; has a long, fast, graceful leap.	Mostly lives by itself in tall jarrah forests of southwest WA; doesn't like thick undergrowth; sometimes feeds with others in early morning and late afternoon; seen out in the day more than most wallabies; rests in the shade during hottest part of day. Land clearing and foxes have wiped out large numbers. Mostly eats grass or grass-like herbs.

Found	Name and Star Quality
	Parma Wallaby (*Macropus parma*) Species is happier in New Zealand than Australia; was once thought extinct, then discovered again.

Looks	Habits
Stands 45–52 cm; weighs 3–6 kg; tail is about same length as its body.	Mostly lives by itself in thick moist forest, or rainforest with open grassy patches; joeys live with their mums; often feeds with others in mob; rests during the day then comes out just before dusk to eat; eats grass, or grass-like herbs. They are great leapers, going very fast with their bodies stretched out to an almost straight line and tails in a straight line behind them.

Index

A
Agile Wallaby (*Macropus agilis*) 21
ant larvae 32
Antilopene Wallaroo 218–219 *see also* wallaroo (*walarro*)
art of indigenous people 35
Australian continent 1–2, 80
Australian languages 44

B
babies *see* joeys
Bald Island (WA) 88
Banded Hare-wallaby (*Lagostrophus fasciatus*) 41
Banks, Sir Joseph 42
barbed-wire 194 *see also* fencing
Batavia (Dutch ship) 39
Bennett's Tree-kangaroo (*Dendrolagus bennettianus*) 80–84, 220–221
Bennett's Wallaby 63
Biceps (wallaby) 15
Big Bum (wallaby) 15
big Red Kangaroo (*Macropus rufus*) 6, 53, 60–63, 124, 141, 149, 169
   distribution, looks, and habits 59, 216–217
   indigenous names 45
Black-footed Rock Wallaby (*Petrogale lateralis*) 92–93, 224–225
Black-gloved Wallaby (*Macropus irma*) 228–229
Black-striped Wallaby (*Macropus dorsalis*) 228–229
Black-tailed Wallaby 6, 65 *see also* Swamp Wallaby
Black Wallaby 65 *see also* Swamp Wallaby
Black Wallaroo 218–219 *see also* wallaroo (*walarro*)
   indigenous names 45
blindness 68, 69
blood 35
blue flier 60

bores 49, 89
Botany Bay 42
Bounce (wallaby) 15
boxing kangaroos 51, 57, 163
breeding and birth
  baby milk 125
  embryos 124
  birth of the joey 122–124
  life inside the pouch 124–127
  world outside the pouch 127–130
  big Reds 62–63, 122
  Eastern Greys 58, 122
  Euros 122
  Quokkas 88
  Red-necked Wallaby 65
  Swamp Wallaby 74–75, 122
  Tammar Wallaby 102
Bridled Nailtail Wallaby (*Onychogalea fraenata*) 4, 97–98
Brush-tailed Rock Wallaby (*Petrogale penicillata*) 93, 226–227
Bush Heritage Fund 198
bushfires 165, 191, 199

C

China, kangaroos in 40
climate change 20, 89, 99
cloaks *see* fur cloaks
Common Wallaroo 218–219 *see also* wallaroo (*walarro*)
Cook, Captain James 41–44
cooling system 141, 145, 148–150
Crescent Nailtail Wallaby (*Onychogalea lunata*) 97
culling 193

D

Dampier, William 41
dams 49, 193
dancing 202, 204
dingoes 31, 48, 127
Diprotodon 20
dogs 70–72, 127, 155, 178, 180, 183, 191, 193
  droppings 137
  Imma 203–204
domesticated animals 39, 164
droppings 131–140
  cat 137
  colour 138–139
  for digestion 4
  dog 137
  farming methods 193
  goat 97, 138
  handling 135
  identifying 136–139
  kangaroo 136–139
  making a collection 139
  rabbit 97, 138, 194
  science and 140
  sheep 136, 138
  wallaby 136–139
  wombat 137
  Quokkas 137
  Rock Wallabies 96–97
drought 2, 32, 118, 141, 148, 193, 197 *see also* water, waterholes
ducks 26–27
dung *see* droppings
dung beetles 131–132

E

earth ovens 34–35
Eastern Grey Kangaroo (*Macropus giganteus*) 54–59,

Eastern Grey Kangaroo
(continued)
112–113, 122, 124
distribution, looks, and
habits 54, 59, 216–217
humans feeding 157–161
indigenous names 44
endangered and threatened
species 4, 52 *see also* extinct
species
Brush-tailed Rock Wallaby
93
Parma Wallaby (vulnerable
species) 103
Rock Wallabies 89–91
Tree-kangaroos 84
Endeavour Reef (Cooktown)
43
Endeavour (ship) 42
energy efficiency 2, 141–142,
145
Eora 44
European records of kangaroos
39–41
Euros *see* wallaroo (*walarro*)
extinct species 97–98, 103
eyes 174–176

F
farmers 3–4, 48–50, 52
living with roos on farms
192–194
farming methods 32, 33, 193
fear 149, 171, 173–177
feet
kangaroos and wallabies 8–9
macropods 10
Quokkas 85
Rock Wallabies 96
Tree-kangaroos 81

female kangaroos and
wallabies *see also* joeys
female joeys 130
in mobs 55
mothers 4, 121
number of teats 121, 128
protecting the joey 127, 164
big Reds 60, 62–63
Swamp Wallaby 68
fencing 49, 55, 185, 194
feral animals 86, 89, 90, 97, 99,
137–138, 168, 191 *see also*
foxes
Fern Wallaby 65 *see also*
Swamp Wallaby
fire-stick farming 31, 33
firelighting 134
Flinders Island 99
food and feeding *see also* water,
waterholes
bad foods 159, 162, 164
in droppings 132–133
feeding wild animals
157–161, 164–165
joeys 125–126
planted grasses 49, 156, 188
preferences 6, 194
on road verges 120, 191, 192
storing 2
times for 170
big Reds 62
Eastern Greys 58
Nabarlek 91
Quokkas 86–88
Rock Wallabies 95
Swamp Wallaby 73, 75–76
Tammar Wallaby 101
foxes 90, 99, 100–101, 168, 191
see also feral animals
introduction of 89

Fred (wallaby) 12–13
fur cloaks 37, 38, 103
Fuschia (roo) 199–204
Fuzz (wallaby) 77–79

G
games 37, 105
gardens 196–197
George III, King of England 46
giant extinct creatures 20
giant roo fossils 18
Giant Short-faced Kangaroo (*Procoptodon goliah*) 17–20
glue 134
goat droppings 97, 138
grasshoppers 193
Grey, Sir George 100, 103
guts 33–34
Guugu Yimithirr (language) 43–44

H
habitat 6, 155–156
habits *see* social groups
Hare-wallaby (*Lagorchestes* species) 222–223
Harry (wallaby) 69–73
Herbert's Rock Wallaby (*Petrogale herberti*) 93
Hop-a-long (wallaby) 15–16
hopping, jumping and bounding
  energy efficiency 2, 141–142, 145
  joeys 129
  kangaroos and wallabies 9
  speed 143, 144, 145
  walking 143
  Eastern Greys 54–55

Parma Wallaby 104
Quokkas 85
Rock Wallabies 96, 111
Swamp Wallaby 74
Tree-kangaroos 81–82
horses 145
House Mouse (wallaby) 15
Houtman Abrolhos (WA) 102
humans
  attacked by roos 162–163, 165, 166
  feeding wild animals 157–161, 164–165
  finding your way around at night 171–173
  gardens 196–197
  good manners around roos and wallabies 162–166, 178
  keeping roos as pets 195
  living with roos on farms 192–194
  locating roos and wallabies 168–171
  roos on the road 192
  senses 172–173
  staring 164, 174, 178
  sweating 149
  wild animals and 89, 155–156
hunting
  colonial dishes 46–48
  for dog meat 193
  human eyes 174–176
  by indigenous people 25–31, 167
  by non-indigenous people 90, 114–115, 179
  by professional shooters 52
hunting nets 29

I

Idalia National Park (Q'ld) 98
indigenous people
  art 35
  firelighting 134
  food 25–26
  hunting 26–31, 167
  laws 27, 35
  names *see* naming of kangaroos and wallabies
Innes National Park (SA) 100–101

J

Jo Jo (roo) 22–24
joeys
  birth of 122–124
  caring for orphans 179–185, 199
  digestion 4
  life inside the pouch 124–127
  marsupial teats 182, 184–185, 186
  milk formula 186
  older joeys 184
  pink joeys 183–184
  temperatures 183–184
  world outside the pouch 127–130
  big Reds 63
  Eastern Greys 58
  Quokkas 88
  Swamp Wallaby 75–76

K

kangaroo apples 205
kangaroo fly 208
kangaroo grass (*Themeda triandra*) 207
Kangaroo Island (WA) 99
kangaroo paws (plants) 205
kangaroo-skin products 37
kangaroos compared with wallabies 6 *see also* wallaby (*wulaba, Wallabia*)
Kangaroos (North Melbourne AFL) 45
kanguru 43
Kawau Island (NZ) 100, 103–104
koalas 122
Kurnai footballs 37

L

laws
  of indigenous people 27, 35
  permits for wildlife carers 181, 195
  for protection of native animals 52
licking paws and wrists *see* cooling system
life span 58, 130
living larders 32
local councils 183
Lumholtz's Tree-kangaroo (*Dendrolagus lumholtzi*) 80–84, 220–221
lumpy jaw 164

M

macropods 8–9
maggots 189
male kangaroos and wallabies 4, 20, 55–57, 68, 112–113, 130
marsupials 1, 8
meat *see* hunting
meat-eating kangaroos 76

Merry Beach (NSW) 148
milk 125, 128
mobs *see* social groups
Monarto Zoological Gardens 101
mutton 48

N

Nabarlek (*Petrogale concinna*) 6, 91–92, 224–225
Nailtail Wallaby (*Onychogalea* species) 97, 150, 222–223
naming of kangaroos and wallabies
  by Europeans 66
  indigenous names 44, 45, 80, 92
  Quokkas 85
  Tree-kangaroos 80
national emblem 3, 54
national parks 50, 98, 100–101, 168, 183, 198
nature reserves 168
nematodes 193
New Guinea *see* Papua New Guinea
New Holland 41–42
New Zealand 100, 103
night sight 172
nocturnal animals 170–171
Northern Nailtail Wallaby (*Onychogalea urguifera*) 97
Nuisance (orphan) 185–190

P

Pademelon (*Thylogale stigmatica, T. thetis, T. billardierii*) 226–227
Pansy (Swampy) 106–110
panting 149

Papua New Guinea 1, 8, 80
Parma Wallaby (*Macropus parma*) 103–104, 230–231
Pebbly Beach (NSW) 148, 157
Pelsart, FranÁois 39–40
pit traps 29
police 183
population numbers 20, 48–50
possums 26, 37, 137
pouches 3, 8, 58, 122, 124–127, 184
Procoptodon see Giant Short-faced Kangaroo (*Procoptodon goliah*)
Prosperpine Rock Wallaby (*Petrogale persephone*) 93, 226–227
protection of native animals 52

Q

Quokka (*Setonix brachyurus*) 41, 85–88, 150, 218–219
  droppings 137

R

rabbit damage 193–194
rabbit droppings 97, 138, 194
rain, hail and thunderstorms 150, 151–154, 171
rare species 139
Rat-Kangaroo fossils 18
Red Kangaroo *see* big Red Kangaroo (*Macropus rufus*)
Red-necked Wallaby (*Macropus rufogriseus*) 6, 63–65, 112, 218–219
road verges 120, 191, 192
roadkill 3, 179, 199
Rock Wallabies 89–97, 111, 124, 150, 169

indigenous names 45
roo jokes 209–214
roo phrases 205–208
roo poo *see* droppings
Rosie (wallaby) 15, 68, 74–75, 77–79
Rottnest Island (WA) 41, 85, 86–88
Royal Australian Air Force (RAAF) 51
Royal National Park (NSW) 50

S
Sahul 80
scats *see* droppings
scent and smell 173, 177, 198
scouts 156
seasons 170
sheep droppings 136, 138
Short-tailed Wallaby (\i1 Setonix brachyurus\i0) 41 *see also* Quokka
sinews 35–37
size 6, 7, 60, 63–64
 of droppings 136
sleeping 119, 148
smell and scent 173, 177, 198
snakes 109, 146
snow 171
social groups
 mobs 6
 territory 144
 big Reds 53, 62
 Eastern Greys 55, 112–113
 Parma Wallaby 104
 Red-necked Wallaby 64
 Rock Wallabies 95
 Swamp Wallaby 73, 109
 Tammar Wallaby 102
 Tree-kangaroos 82–84

soil 32
Solander, Dr 42
sounds 203
spotlighting 170
stinker roos 59
Stinkers 65
superphosphate 49
Swamp Wallaby (*Wallabia bicolor*) 65–68, 109, 124, 150, 220–221
 indigenous names 44
sweating 118, 149
swimming 144, 148

T
tails
 for balance 9, 142
 Nailtail Wallabies 98
 Quokkas 85
 Rock Wallabies 93–95
 Swamp Wallaby 75
 tracks 146–147
 of Tree-kangaroos 81
Tammar Wallaby (*Macropus eugenii*) 40, 98–103, 124
 distribution, looks, and habits 98, 228–229
 indigenous names 45, 99
 milk 128
Tasman, Captain Abel 40
Tasmania 63, 65 *see also* Van Diemen's Land
Taunton National Park (Scientific, Q'ld) 98
Terra Australis Incognita 41–42
territory 144
threatened species *see* endangered and threatened species
torches 172

toxoplasmosis 90
tracks 30, 146–147
tree climbing 86, 96
Tree-kangaroos 80–84, 144

V

Van Diemen's Land 46 *see also* Tasmania
Vlamingh, Willem de 85
Volkerson, Samuel 41
Volkertzoon, Samuel 85

W

Wallabies (rugby union team) 45
wallaby (*wulaba, Wallabia*)
  compared with kangaroos 6
  culling 193
  droppings 136–139
  fur 65, 66, 93, 103
  gardens 196–197
  lost colonies 97–98
  as meat 47
  milk 128
  naming 45, 66
  population 50
  species 105
  tracks 146–147
  use of camouflage 169, 176–177
wallaroo (*walarro*) 45, 122, 150, 218–219
Warabi Wallaby (*Petrogale burbidgei*) 53, 91, 92, 222–223
water, waterholes 29, 102, 108, 109, 169 *see also* drought; food and feeding
Western Brush Wallaby (*Macropus irma*) 228–229
Western Grey Kangaroo (*Macropus fuliginosus*) 59, 122, 124, 216–217
Whiptail Wallaby 43–44
Wildcare 181
wildlife carers 181–183, 195
wildlife courses 184
wildlife preservation 198–199
wire fencing *see* fencing
WIRES 181
wombats 69–70, 120, 122, 137, 146, 179, 198
wounds 189

Y

Yellow-footed Rock Wallaby (*Petrogale xanthopus*) 4, 93, 224–225
Yellowstone National Park (US) 50

WIRES (Wildlife Information and Rescue Service) is the largest wildlife rescue and rehabilitation organisation in Australia. If you have an injured animal,
phone 1800 641 188 (free call).
If you would like to know more about WIRES or require information for school projects,
visit their website at www.wires.org.au

Australian Fauna Care has a list of all licensed organisations that help injured wildlife in Australia. To find a wildlife carer near you, phone (02) 4446 0835 or send an e-mail to info@fauna.org.au, or visit their website at www.fauna.org.au

Farming and wildlife: see Jackie's website at
www.jackiefrench.com
Register for her free monthly newsletter at
www.harpercollins.com.au/jackiefrench

The Secret World of Wombats

JACKIE FRENCH

BRUCE WHATLEY

*Underneath your feet is a strange new world . . .
the world of wombats!*

Jackie French has been living with and studying wombats for over thirty years — they are her Muse for many wonderful stories she has written.

Now, Jackie has put down almost everything anyone ever wanted to know about wombats — especially *her* wombats! To Jackie wombats are more fascinating even than aliens — and just as strange!

Discover why wombats bite each other's bums. How wombats 'speak' to each other with their wombat droppings. How can you care for an orphan wombat. And how you too can get close to wombats!

Jackie French is a full-time writer and wombat negotiator. Jackie writes fiction and non-fiction for all ages, and has columns in the print media. Jackie is regarded as one of Australia's most popular children's authors. She writes across all genres — from picture books, humour and history to science fiction.

Visit Jackie's websites

www.jackiefrench.com

or

www.harpercollins.com.au/jackiefrench
to subscribe to her monthly newsletter

Some of Jackie's Awards

The Secret World of Wombats
- Shortlisted for The Wilderness Society's non-fiction book award in the Environment Award for Children's Literature 2006
- Shortlisted for the Patricia Wrightson prize in the 2006 NSW Premier's Literary Awards

Hitler's Daughter
- CBC Younger Readers' Award winner, 2000
- UK National Literacy Association WOW! Award winner, 2001
- Shortlisted in the Fiction for Older Readers category, YABBA awards 2007
- US Library Association Notable Book
- Koala Awards 2007, Roll of Honour
- Semi-Grand Prix award, Japan
- The Helpmann Award for a Children's Presentation and two Drover's Awards, 2007, for the Monkey Baa production of *Hitler's Daughter: the play*

In Your Blood
- ACT Book of the Year, 2002

Diary of a Wombat (illustrated by Bruce Whatley)
- Nielsen BookData/Australian Booksellers Association Book of the Year, 2002 (the only picture book ever to win this award)
- (USA) Benjamin Franklin Award
- (USA) Lemmee Award
- (USA) Favourite Picture Book of the Year, Cuffie Awards, 2003
- (USA) Funniest Book in the Cuffie Awards (tied with *Diary of a Worm*), 2003
- Cool Award, for Best Picture Book, voted by the kids of the ACT, 2003
- Young Australian Readers' Award winner, 2003
- KOALA Award for Best Picture Book winner, 2003

- (USA) KIND Award winner, 2004
- Shortlisted for the Bilby Awards, 2007
- Northern Territory KROC Award for Favourite Book of 2007

To the Moon and Back (co-written with Bryan Sullivan, Jackie's husband)
- CBC Eve Pownall Award for Information Books winner, 2005

They Came on Viking Ships
- Shortlisted: (UK) Essex Book Award; winner to be announced in 2008
- Winner: West Australian Young Readers' Book Awards (WAYBRA) (Younger Readers), 2007
- Shortlisted: NSW Premier's History Awards (Young People's History Prize), 2006

Macbeth and Son
- Shortlisted: CBC Awards, 2007

The Goat Who Sailed the World
- Notable Book: CBC Awards (Younger Readers), 2007

Josephine Wants To Dance (illustrated by Bruce Whatley)
- Australian Booksellers' Book of the Year, Younger Readers, 2007.
- Notable Book: CBC Awards (Early Childhood), 2007
- Notable Book: CBC Awards (Picture Book of the Year), 2007

Pharaoh
- Shortlisted: CBC Awards (Older Readers), 2008

Shaggy Gully Times (illustrated by Bruce Whatley)
- Shortlisted: CBC Awards (Younger Readers), 2008

Other Titles by Jackie French

Wacky Families Series
1. My Dog the Dinosaur • 2. My Mum the Pirate • 3. My Dad the Dragon
4. My Uncle Gus the Garden Gnome • 5. My Uncle Wal the Werewolf
6. My Gran the Gorilla • 7. My Auntie Chook the Vampire Chicken
8. My Pa the Polar Bear

Phredde Series
1. A Phaery Named Phredde • 2. Phredde and a Frog Named Bruce
3. Phredde and the Zombie Librarian • 4. Phredde and the Temple of Gloom
5. Phredde and the Leopard-Skin Librarian • 6. Phredde and the Purple Pyramid
7. Phredde and the Vampire Footy Team • 8. Phredde and the Ghostly Underpants

Outlands Trilogy
In the Blood • Blood Moon • Flesh and Blood

Historical
Somewhere Around the Corner • Dancing with Ben Hall • Soldier on the Hill
Daughter of the Regiment • Hitler's Daughter • Lady Dance • The White Ship
How the Finnegans Saved the Ship • Valley of Gold • Tom Appleby, Convict Boy
They Came on Viking Ships • Macbeth and Son • Pharaoh
The Goat who Sailed the World • The Dog who Loved a Queen
A Rose for the Anzac Boys

Fiction
Rain Stones • Walking the Boundaries • The Secret Beach • Summerland
Beyond the Boundaries • A Wombat Named Bosco • The Book of Unicorns
The Warrior – The Story of a Wombat • Tajore Arkle • Missing You, Love Sara
Dark Wind Blowing • Ride the Wild Wind: The Golden Pony and Other Stories

Non-fiction
Seasons of Content • How the Aliens from Alpha Centauri Invaded
My Maths Class and Turned Me into a Writer
How to Guzzle Your Garden • The Book of Challenges
Stamp, Stomp, Whomp • The Fascinating History of Your Lunch
Big Burps, Bare Bums and Other Bad-Mannered Blunders
To the Moon and Back • Rocket Your Child into Reading
The Secret World of Wombats
The Wonderful World of Wallabies and Kangaroos

Picture Books
Diary of a Wombat • Pete the Sheep • Josephine Wants to Dance
The Shaggy Gully Times